'After centuries of obscuration, the priceless treasures of the Islamic civilisation are finally being unearthed little by little. The treasure this timely book succeeds to bring to light is the Islamic pattern of holistic healthcare in general and mental healthcare in particular, the latter being a first in the history of civilisation. Of utmost interest is the ability of mediaeval physicians to harness every possible resource in their environment, thereby achieving truly remarkable results.'

—**Dr. Mostafa al-Badawi**, *Consultant Psychiatrist and Author of, among other titles,* Man and the Universe and Spiritual Significance in Islamic Architecture

'In the late 1970s, I had a chance encounter with a German engineer. In a remote area where he was building a road in Iran, he had come upon a mediaeval mental hospital, still running on its original endowment, that treated mental disorders, not with Western pharmacology, but through architecture!—the colour blue, a "golden ratio" in proportions, a "mandala" courtyard, fountains. The effect, he said, was so tranquillising that he decided to stay and had "the best night's sleep in my life"'.

'His account intrigued me. In the 45-odd years since, I was, however, able to discover only a little about early Muslim mental hospitals—until reading Rania Awaad and Merve Nursoy-Demir's ground-breaking edited book.

This is a "must read" book for anyone with an interest in Islamic Psychology, but it should appeal to a much wider readership and has the force itself to encourage a paradigm shift in how we in the West view mental illness and its treatment.'

—**Dr. Rasjid E. Skinner**, *Clinical Director at Ihsaan Therapeutic Services and Visiting Professor at International Islamic University Islamabad*

'A vital contribution to the field of Islamic psychology. Looking to the past to elucidate the profound wisdom and practical methods used by Islamic institutions of holistic, community healthcare, the authors reveal how relevant and needed such practices are today. Despite advancements in modern medicine, there have been major side effects, including the disaggregation of body and soul and disconnection from nature and community. The future of Islamic psychology, and health and wellbeing more broadly, requires efforts to "catch up with the past", reviving traditional healing practices and institutions tailored to modern circumstances. This book is a crucial step towards that future.'

—**Dr. Abdallah Rothman**, *Clinical Director of DAR al-Shifaa and Executive Director of the International Association of Islamic Psychology*

Maristāns and Islāmic Psychology

Maristāns and Islāmic Psychology outlines how the novel methods, tools, and approaches for treating psychological illnesses developed in the maristāns (hospitals) of the Muslim world can be utilised today in formulating a practical implementation of Islāmic psychology (IP). As a trademark of the Islāmic civilisation, the maristāns were institutions of healing that boasted the world's first treatment centres for treating psychological illnesses. They also served as the centres where theoretical concepts developed by early Muslim scholars—physicians, theologians, and philosophers—who contributed to the creation of IP were translated into practical, clinical applications.

A detailed examination of the treatment modalities within these historical treatment centres provides a promising model for creating a holistic approach to psychological healing that is grounded in Islāmic heritage. This text completes such an examination, highlighting the practical IP treatment methods in fourteen maristāns geographically spread throughout the Muslim world in order to bridge this centuries-long model of psychological care to the modern context.

As part of the Islāmic Psychology and Psychotherapy Focus series, this book provides a foundation for mental health professionals who either directly deliver mental health services or are involved in creating theories, institutions, or spaces of IP and psychotherapeautic practices.

Dr. Rania Awaad, MD, is a Clinical Professor of Psychiatry at the Stanford University School of Medicine, USA, where she is the Director of the Stanford Muslim Mental Health & Islāmic Psychology Lab. In the community, she serves as the President of Maristān, a holistic mental health non-profit organisation serving Muslim communities, and the Director of The Rahmah Foundation, a non-profit organisation dedicated to educating Muslim women and girls. Follow her @Dr.RaniaAwaad.

Merve Nursoy-Demir, MA, obtained her bachelor's degrees in the Departments of Psychology and History at Bogazici University, Istanbul, Turkey. Upon completing her master's degree in Clinical Psychology at Bahcesehir University, Istanbul, Merve started working in the Stanford Muslim Mental Health and Islāmic Psychology Lab. Currently, her research topics are on mental health practices, institutions, and theories in Islāmic history.

Focus Series on Islāmic Psychology and Psychotherapy

Series Editor: Professor Dr. G. Hussein Rassool, Professor of Islāmic Psychology

About the Series

In contemporary times, there is increasing focus on the need to adapt approaches of psychology, counselling psychology and psychotherapy to accommodate the integration of spirituality and psychology. With the increasing focus on the need to meet the holistic needs of Muslims, there was a call to adapt approaches to the understanding of behaviour and experiences from an Islāmic epistemological and ontological worldview.

The aim of the Focus Series on Islāmic psychology and psychotherapy is to introduce a range of educational, clinical and research interventions relating to Islāmic psychology and psychotherapy that are authentic, practical, concise, and based on cutting-edge research. Each volume focuses on a particular aspect of Islāmic psychology and psychotherapy, its application with a specific client group, a particular methodology or approach, or a critical analysis of existing and emergent theoretical and historical ideas.

Each book in the Focus Series is written, in accessible language, with the assumption that the readers have no prior knowledge of Islāmic psychology and psychotherapy.

Islāmically Modified Cognitive Behavioural Therapy (2025)
By Mahdi Qasqas

Tazkiya Therapy in Islāmic Psychotherapy (2025)
Bagus Riyono

Maristāns and Islāmic Psychology
A Historical Model for Modern Implementation
Rania Awaad and Merve Nursoy-Demir

Maristāns and Islāmic Psychology

A Historical Model for Modern Implementation

Rania Awaad and Merve Nursoy-Demir

Routledge
Taylor & Francis Group
LONDON AND NEW YORK

First published 2025
by Routledge
4 Park Square, Milton Park, Abingdon, Oxon OX14 4RN

and by Routledge
605 Third Avenue, New York, NY 10158

Routledge is an imprint of the Taylor & Francis Group, an informa business

British Library Cataloguing-in-Publication Data
A catalogue record for this book is available from the British Library

Library of Congress Cataloging-in-Publication Data
Names: Awaad, Rania, author. | Nursoy-Demir, Merve, author.
Title: Maristāns and Islāmic psychology : a historical model for modern implementation / Rania Awaad and Merve Nursoy-Demir.
Description: Abingdon, Oxon ; New York, NY : Routledge, 2025. | Series: Islamic psychology and psychotherapy series | Includes bibliographical references and index.
Identifiers: LCCN 2024038103 (print) | LCCN 2024038104 (ebook) | ISBN 9781032359694 (hardback) | ISBN 9781032359687 (paperback) | ISBN 9781003329589 (ebook)
Subjects: LCSH: Islam—Psychology. | Psychotherapy—Religious aspects—Islam.
Classification: LCC BP175 .A925 2025 (print) | LCC BP175 (ebook) | DDC 297.2/615—dc23/eng/20241021
LC record available at https://lccn.loc.gov/2024038103
LC ebook record available at https://lccn.loc.gov/2024038104

ISBN: 9781032359694 (hbk)
ISBN: 9781032359687 (pbk)
ISBN: 9781003329589 (ebk)

DOI: 10.4324/9781003329589

Typeset in Times New Roman
by codeMantra

بسم الله الرحمن الرحيم

This book is dedicated to Anse Sawsan Imady, who took me (RA) to visit my first maristān in Damascus, Syria, when I was a teenager. Her teachings about the interdisciplinary and interconnected aspects of human healing forever planted the seed of love and curiosity in my heart, ultimately leading me on this journey to revive the holistic healing potential of the maristāns in the modern era.

Contents

Foreword

'Maristān' comes from the Persian word 'bīmaristān', meaning place for treating the sick. Maristāns were renowned hospitals in the early Islāmic world, providing care and treatment irrespective of the patient's religion or social status, and treating mental as well as physical conditions.

The earliest mention of maristāns dates as far back as the end of the first Islāmic century in Damascus during the reign of the Umayyad caliph Walīd ibn 'Abd al-Malik (d. 715). They offered a broad range of support services, such as the provision of boarding and lodging, in addition to the medical care from trained professional staff. Maristāns also served as hubs for the growth of medical knowledge and research which then spread into Europe during its Middle Ages. Though maristāns as such do not exist today, they are an important part of the Islāmic world's cultural heritage and its particular contribution to the field of medicine and medical research.

These historically significant centres of healthcare and medicine need and deserve to be studied in the context of global medical history. Although in recent years, there has been some progress in this area, specialist attention to the disciplines underpinning the work of the maristāns remains regrettably rare.

My knowledge of this field is limited and so I was deeply grateful for the opportunity to read through a draft of Dr. Rania Awaad's forthcoming book, *Maristāns and Islāmic Psychology: A Historical Model for Modern Implementation*. I found this to be a very impressive work, the result of assiduous attention to the relevant primary sources. It will prove to be a significant milestone in the exploration of maristān healthcare within the broader context of global medical history. It sheds light especially on the invaluable contributions of maristāns to the development of IP and to the relevance worldwide, and in our time, of Islāmic approaches to the conception and treatment of mental illness.

How did Islam view mental illness? What did early Muslim physicians say about mental health? These and similar questions led Awaad to many years of tracking and gathering manuscript materials from the 8th century through to the 13th century and thereafter. She examined records of medical research in different libraries around the world. Her research has demonstrated that Muslim physicians discussed mental illness at length and were highly sophisticated in their approach to identifying and diagnosing mental illnesses and proposing courses of treatment. In some cases, their classifications, diagnosis, and treatment plans closely match DSM-5 criteria and recommendations (p. 3).

Awaad further says (p. 3): '...many types of scholars beyond physicians contributed to the field of psychology, known in early Muslim societies as *Ilm al-Nafs* (the Science of the Self). The field was quite interdisciplinary, with physicians, theologians, and philosophers all contributing'. The co-operation across disciplines and the reciprocated benefits of such co-operation are among several features that set IP apart from Western psychology. After spending some years working through the manuscripts of the great thinkers and contributors to the Islāmic legacy, Awaad realised that 'these individuals did not work in [separate] silos. In fact, many of them were practising physicians who directed or worked in the hospitals of their time. This next stage of my research was as much eye-opening as it was awe-inspiring. In the same way that early Muslims instituted *masājid* (places of worship) everywhere Islam spread, they also established two other important institutions: *madāris* (schools for teaching Islāmic sciences) and maristāns (hospitals)' (p. 4).

This is a well-structured book, arranged in seven comprehensive and coherent chapters. These chapters discuss different aspects of mental healthcare in the maristāns: the introduction of these hospitals; the financial systems supporting them; the multidisciplinary teams involved in patient care; and the organisational structures ensuing their maintenance and continuance. The treatment methods and approaches used in maristāns are compared with modern psychiatric practices, highlighting the diversity within the historical spectrum of treatment. Also presented are the locations of maristāns, including architectural and landscape features selected for their affect on the delivery of mental healthcare. In an overview from a clinician's perspective Dr Awaad surveys the holistic care offered in maristāns, picking out in particular those elements that could be reintegrated into contemporary clinical practice, notably under the rubric of integrative psychiatry.

She also discusses modern mental health centres like the Maristān or Khalil Center as examples of practical efforts made to revive the Islāmic heritage in mental healthcare, and to bridge historical and contemporary needs and practices. Her purpose in showing parallels (as well as divergences) between past and present is to contribute to the improvement of mental healthcare through a comprehensive understanding of both traditional and modern approaches. This approach enables a more rounded understanding of what maristāns were trying to do and a deeper appreciation of the complexities inherent in this topic.

Awaad's focus on maristāns and their relationship with IP builds a unique perspective that highlights the intersection of healthcare, spirituality, and cultural practices. Through her research, she both honours the legacy of maristāns and provides insights that can inform contemporary approaches to healthcare delivery and psychological well-being.

As its title indicates, Awaad's work, with its emphasis on 'modern implementation', means that she has gone beyond historical analysis to encompass a possible practical application of that analysis. Evidently, her position is that lessons can be learned from maristān healthcare practices that are relevant for and applicable to present-day healthcare systems. She writes:

This exploration of the Islāmic world's maristāns reveals far more than a series of historical footnotes in healthcare. These institutions, scattered across a vast geographical landscape and spanning centuries, were not mere anomalies of generosity or progressive thought. Instead, they stand as towering testaments to a profound and shared ethos within the Islāmic civilisation—a conviction that providing unconditional care to the destitute and afflicted is not just an act of charity but a fundamental expression of piety and profound human empathy. This ethos was embraced by governments, rulers, and philanthropists alike, who saw in these maristāns an opportunity to leave a lasting mark of compassion and societal advancement. The striking commonalities among these maristāns—in their treatment methodologies, architectural elegance, and operational blueprints—reveal a deeply ingrained philosophy of care that transcended regional and chronological borders. These maristāns were much more than healthcare centres; they were beacons of hope and healing hubs that uplifted entire communities, enhancing the quality of life for residents and weary travellers alike. They not only secured the legacy of their patrons but also etched an enduring narrative of benevolence and welfare in the annals of Islāmic history. (pp. 60–61)

The normalisation of mental healthcare in both the public realm and the medical realm for all beneficiaries of maristāns, including 'women and men, old and young, free and enslaved' (waqf deed of Qalāwūn Maristān as cited in Issa 1981, p. 87), serves as a model for our time. Furthermore, the attitudes of some leading scholars of the time towards psychologically disturbed patients offer a unique approach that avoids making the patient feel like an anomaly. For example, al-Balkhī would refer to neurotic patients as 'a person whose emotional overreactions have become a habit' (al-Balkhi & Badri, 2013, p. 14), implying that their inherent identity was not bound to their illness. Instead, he identified it as a temporary and mutable condition. By integrating a humanising mindset within modern psychotherapeutic models, we can begin to make clinical mental healthcare more approachable for diverse patient populations. (p. 119)

I am profoundly grateful to Dr. Awaad for this outstanding contribution to our knowledge and understanding of maristāns, both their historical roles and their modern relevance. Her insights shed the most welcome light on a vital aspect of Islāmic history and culture that has been relatively neglected.

She might never have undertaken this work, let alone brought it to such a high degree of realisation, but for her appreciation of what inspired Muslims to build and improve maristāns. In her own words:

Islāmic teachings were the primary source of inspiration, the impetus for creating a model that historically led to holistic healing in maristāns. The false dichotomy of separating religious and 'secular' sciences that exists today in professionals' minds did not exist in the era of the maristāns. We argue that the field of human psychology will only be complete enough to provide in-depth healing to not only Muslims but people in general when Islāmic conceptualisations of human ontology, health, and illness are bridged to modern clinical practice (pp. 198–99).

Mohammad Akram Nadwi
Oxford, UK
February 2024

Preface

I (RA), like many Muslims living in the modern era, had never heard of the connection between mental health and Islam. I consider myself a product of the communities that raised me. The stigma against mental health in these otherwise nurturing communities was palpable, and this meant that I, too, held internalised stigmas towards the fields of psychology and psychiatry. It was only during the later stages of my medical school studies that I witnessed many mental health-related incidents as a teacher of the Islāmic sacred sciences (which I was engaged in alongside my college and medical studies). This made me realise that the very Muslim communities that I served and cherished were suffering from not openly addressing mental illness. I made a last-minute switch to psychiatry for my postgraduate residency training, which took place at Stanford University. When I arrived at Stanford, I was quite suspicious about the entire field. I knew I wanted to help Muslim communities, but I questioned my place in the mental health world as an observant Muslim. Questions welled in my mind: what does Islam say about mental illness? How did our noble predecessors understand mental health? Surely, with all of their advancements in the sciences, medicine, and humanities, the early Muslims must have also contributed to the mental health field!

These questions led me to a deep dive that spanned multiple years of gathering manuscripts dating back to Islāmic antiquity, from as early as the 8th century through the 16th century onwards. At first, I (RA) checked out medical manuscripts from the Stanford Libraries and eventually from around the country and world using the interlibrary loan system. I quickly realised that not only did Muslim physicians write about mental illness, but they also innovated sophisticated diagnostic classifications for mental illness and suggested a myriad of treatment modalities. In some cases, their classifications, diagnoses, and treatment plans were so accurate that they matched today's DSM-5 criteria (see my papers on the likes of al-Balkhī and al-Rāzī). I also discovered that many types of scholars beyond physicians contributed to the field of psychology, known in early Muslim societies as *Ilm al-Nafs* (the Science of the Self). This field was quite interdisciplinary, with physicians, theologians, and philosophers all contributing. These interdisciplinary contributions are among the many aspects that set IP apart from Western psychology. Analysing and translating the works of early Muslim scholars eventually led to the establishment of my lab at Stanford University: The Muslim Mental Health and Islāmic Psychology Lab. My early publications laid the foundation for much more research and discoveries. We were quite literally unearthing findings that were re-writing the history of psychology.

After spending some years reading through the manuscripts of the great thinkers and contributors of the Islāmic heritage, it dawned on me (RA) that these individuals did not work in silos. In fact, many of them were practising physicians who directed or worked in the hospitals of their time. This next stage of my research was as much eye-opening as it was awe-inspiring. In the same way that early Muslims instituted *masājid* (places of worship) everywhere Islam spread, they also established two other important institutions: *madāris* (schools for teaching Islāmic sciences) and maristāns (hospitals). Oftentimes, these three institutions would be part of the same *kulliyah* (complex) along with other institutions such as the *sharābkhānah* (pharmacy), *ḥammām* (bathhouse), *'imārat* (soup kitchen), *zāwiyāh* (spiritual lodge), *ṭab'khānah* (guest house), as well as orchards or a bazaar that served as a revenue-generating facet of the endowed property. Each of these institutions played a part in a holistic healing model the early Muslims understood to be the way to treat an illness, whether physical, mental, or spiritual. This *kulliyah* offered holistic healing for the mind, body, and soul.

The Islāmic hospitals, in particular, were considered 'secular' (i.e., here meaning not governed by religious leaders) institutions that were run by physicians rather than religious leaders (Horden, 1993). This was a major departure from European hospitals or convalescence centres that existed at the same time period. At best, mental illness in Europe's Middle Ages was treated by religious leaders who attributed psychological ailments to supernatural causes (Awaad et al., 2019). At worst, individuals with mental illnesses were burned at the stake, thought to be witches. In contrast, the maristāns of the Muslim world were very likely—to the best of our knowledge and research—the first in the world to establish separate wards for the medicalised treatment of mental illness within the hospital system. Psychiatric illnesses were treated on equal footing to any other physical illness in these maristāns. The psychiatry ward stood side by side with the surgical, obstetrics/gynaecological, ophthalmological, internal medicine, and other specialised wards. This finding proved that mental illnesses were not as heavily stigmatised in early Muslim societies, nor as frequently discriminated against compared to physical illnesses, as we further elaborate in this book. Although 'secular', these maristāns were very much inspired by the teachings of Islam, and Islāmic spirituality played a major role therein. In Persian, these hospitals were called bīmaristāns (literally a place for the sick), and the term was later Latinised to maristāns (which we chose to use in this book). In Arabic, the equivalent term used was *dār al-shifā'* (the abode of healing). Even in its namesake, maristāns focused on healing rather than illness.

Along the way, I (RA) met my co-author, Merve Nursoy-Demir, who was also interested in the historical roots of psychology inspired by the Islāmic tradition. Having trained in Turkey, she spent time looking into the Turkish archives, particularly into Ottoman Music Therapy that the maristāns utilised as a medicinal treatment for psychiatric conditions. As we further delved into our research about the maristāns, we were grateful for the chance to visit several maristāns that are currently still standing, namely in Turkey and Egypt. Much of what we present in this book is the result of years of research into historical manuscripts from Islāmic antiquity combined with visits to currently standing maristāns in order to better understand the unique contributions Muslims made to the field of medicine broadly and to their pioneering advancements to the fields of psychology and psychiatry specifically.

Structure of the Book

This book is composed of seven chapters. The introductory chapter, Chapter 1, presents an overview of the Islāmic roots of psychiatric care by referring to Qur'ānic verses and Ḥadīth that emphasise the importance of (psychological) well-being, seeking cures for diseases, and providing for the needy. In Chapter 2, we introduce fourteen well-known maristāns that provided mental healthcare across the vast geography of Muslim lands, emphasising the features they held in common. In Chapter 3, we introduce the financial system that allowed the hospitals to offer free services, the interdisciplinary teams that delivered treatment and care, and the organisational structure that enabled maintenance. Chapter 4 is devoted entirely to the treatment of patients in maristāns. Here, treatment methods and approaches from a diverse spectrum (e.g., psychopharmacology, music therapy, talk therapy, aromatherapy) are presented in detail. In Chapter 5 we address some of the characteristic features found in the physical environment of maristāns, including their architectural designs, landscape features, locations, and symbolism, all discussed in relation to their effect on mental healthcare. In Chapter 6 we provide a blueprint of the maristān model of holistic care. Here, we explore the elements of maristāns that may be possible to revive within modern-day IP clinical practice. In our concluding chapter, Chapter 7, we provide an overview of the entire book and offer clinical guidelines for aspiring IP clinicians and organisations.

Aim of the Book

We pray that this effort accomplishes the following goals:

1 Helps re-write the history of psychology that is often very narrow and Eurocentric in its approach (Lipsitt, 2003), thereby writing the contributions of Muslims out of its history, whether inadvertently or purposefully (Wright et al., 2012). It is imperative that Muslim communities connect

back to their rich legacy and heritage of holistic well-being that had once led to great strides in mental health. In accordance with scientific citation methods, our aim is to set a precedent for any author who writes about the history of psychiatric hospitals or about the history of psychology to cite our work and thereby allow for the re-writing of a more diverse and less Eurocentric history of psychology.

2 Helps Muslims rightfully re-claim their heritage as it relates to mental health. Many mental health discoveries are often misattributed to and misappropriated by European psychologists, often centuries after they were first discovered and implemented by Muslim scholars. By reconnecting Muslims to their rich heritage and correcting misinformation (such as Berrios's claim that 'Muslims only translated the works of the Greeks and contributed nothing of their own; Porter, 2010), there is a greater possibility of instilling a sense of pride in one's heritage and openness to trying a holistic approach to treating mental illness that was once prevalent in historical Muslim societies. This, in turn, has the ability to reduce modern-day stigma against mental illness.
3 Aids in the rooted revival of the maristāns as a holistic healing institution (Şentürk, 2020). Our hope is that this first book on the maristāns serves as a blueprint for recreating fully functional, modern-day maristāns. Many acknowledge that the modern psychiatric system is broken, and an alternative, more holistic system is needed. The interdisciplinary, holistic healing model of the maristāns has much to offer the modern world. Though we have a good deal of work still ahead of us, we offer this book as a starting point for future revival endeavours.

Disclaimer

This is not a history book, even though we have surveyed and summarised extensive historical literature about Islāmic hospitals. Instead, the current work hopes to serve as a blueprint for an efficient clinical infrastructure that is Islāmically inspired in its essence. As such, our primary goal is to provide a comprehensive survey on maristāns, an institution commonly referred to in the IP field yet requires further elaboration. An in-depth analysis of the psychiatric care that was once offered in these maristāns can provide insights into models of clinical practice for those interested in delivering authentic forms of Islāmic psychotherapy.

Anachronism (i.e., interpretation of a historical phenomenon outside of its temporal context), more specifically a form of anachronism called presentism, is a potential limitation in an interdisciplinary book like ours that utilises historical content. As an approach disregarded by historians for years (Hunt, 2002), presentism can be simply defined as looking into the past through the lens of the present when undertaking historical studies. The majority of historians have claimed that the past should be examined in its own circumstances by keeping a distance from the present. According to this approach, which has been the norm in the field of history for a long time, a clinical discussion of maristāns in the context of today's IP field carries the risk of overstepping that line. However, critics of this form of sterilised study of the past claim that it hinders great growth potential that can aid humanity in shaping the future (Armitage, 2023). We believe in the unravelled potential of maristāns to help future clinical IP practices flourish. Understanding the key elements of an Islāmically inspired mental healthcare system that served efficiently for centuries is too much to lose by remaining sterile.

Two main categories of references—primary and secondary sources—are typically used in historical analyses. Primary sources usually contain first-hand records of people, events, or actions in the form of, for example, contemporary eyewitness accounts that chronicle certain events. This type of source provides an authentic, eye-witness point of view and can usually be found in archives. However, the limited accessibility and readability of primary sources can create a natural challenge to incorporate them directly into research studies. Secondary sources, on the other hand, are reports that refer to or quote from primary sources. To generate the book at hand, we reviewed, translated, and analysed several primary and secondary sources in multiple languages (e.g., Arabic, Turkish, Persian, German, and French). At times when direct access to original, historical documents (i.e., primary sources) was not possible, such as limited access to relevant archives or simply the lack of original manuscripts, we used reliable secondary sources to complete the pieces of this massive puzzle. For the transliteration of non-English words, we used the ALA-LC romanisation style.

Rania Awaad, MD
Merve Nursoy-Demir, MA
Stanford, CA, USA
February, 2024

Acknowledgements

Every success is from Allāh (ﷻ, May His glory be glorified), and every word of *'ilm* (knowledge) is His blessing. *Hamd* (praise) and *shukr* (gratitude) are to Him alone for the gift of *'ilm* and the opportunity to share it with others. We hope and pray to be in His servitude with the works we are involved in academically, clinically, or communally. We also hope and pray that this work will bring our souls closer to the most ideal human of all times, our beloved Prophet Muḥammad (ﷺ, d. 632 CE).

For the formulation and completion of this book, there are multiple individuals to whom we owe our immense appreciation. First and foremost, we would like to thank our editors at Routledge, Professor Hussein Rasool and Grace McDonnell, for their ongoing support and patience during the production of this volume. Their feedback guided our way to a higher quality of the work at hand. Second, this book is the product of a team effort. We would like to thank our colleagues from the Stanford Muslim Mental Health and Islāmic Psychology Lab, especially Nadira Baig for her detailed edits, Danah El-Sayed for her invaluable feedback on the content, and Ayisat Adegbindin for her assistance in the graphic design of the maristāns map. We would like to thank our consultant historian, Professor Mehmet Ipsirli, for the guidance he provided along the way. Lastly, any acknowledgements of our family will be inadequate, by whose support this book became achievable.

Rania Awaad, MD
Merve Nursoy-Demir, MA
Stanford, California
March, 2024

References

Armitage, D. (2023). In defense of presentism. In D. M. McMahon (Ed.), *History and Human Flourishing* (pp. 44–69). Oxford University Press.

Awaad, R., Mohammad, A., Elzamzamy, K., Fereydooni, S., & Gamar, M. (2019). Mental health in the islamic golden era: the historical roots of modern psychiatry.

In H. S. Moffic, J. Peteet, A. Z. Hankir, & R. Awaad (Eds.), *Islamophobia and Psychiatry* (pp. 3–17). Springer. https://doi.org/10.1007/978-3-030-00512-2_1
Horden, P. (1993). Responses to possession and insanity in the earlier byzantine world. *Social History of Medicine*, *6*(2), 177–194. https://doi.org/10.1093/shm/6.2.177
Hunt, L. (2002). Against presentism. *Perspectives on History*, *40*(5), 7–9.
Lipsitt, D. R. (2003). Psychiatry and the general hospital in an age of uncertainty. *World Psychiatry: Official Journal of the World Psychiatric Association (WPA)*, *2*(2), 87–92.
Porter, R. (2010). *Madness: A Brief History.* Nachdr University Press.
Şentürk, R. (2020). *Comparative Theories and Methods: Between Uniplexity and Multiplexity* (1st ed.). İbn Haldun University Press.
Wright, P., Stern, J., & Phelan, M. (2012). *Core Psychiatry* (3rd ed.). Saunders Elsevier.

1 Strong Roots Lead to Blossoming Fruits

Foundations of the Maristāns

Muhammed-Talha Topçu,
Merve Nursoy-Demir and Rania Awaad

Introduction

As we enter the dawn of the revival of Islāmic psychology (IP), it is of utmost importance to access reliable knowledge about the preceding theories and practices of psychology from the Islāmic intellectual heritage. While numerous attempts to create Islāmically oriented clinical interventions or psychological approaches have emerged around the globe in the last decade (Kaplick & Skinner, 2017; Al-Karam, 2018; Isgandarova, 2019; Keshavarzi et al., 2020; Keshavarzi & Haque, 2013; Rothman & Coyle, 2018; Rassool, 2021), it is imperative to establish a comprehensive understanding of the historical origins of Islāmic psychological healing methods in order to appropriately facilitate a rooted revival (Şentürk, 2020) of this incredible holistic healing system. The acknowledgement of Islam's historical heritage is a necessary first step—not simply to romanticise a glorious, feel-good past but to accurately conceptualise, theorise, and practically implement clinical perspectives that are rooted in the Islāmic tradition. Today, many Muslim communities worldwide suffer from the stigmatisation of mental health on multiple levels, which contributes to the inaccessibility of mental health services, including psychotherapy, even though Muslims may need mental healthcare services more than ever due to war, refugee status, forced displacement, Islamophobia, and multiple other disadvantaged living conditions (Ali-Faisal, 2020; Elkassem et al., 2018; Shoib et al., 2022).

The colonisation of medical and psychological knowledge, and more importantly, the colonisation of the minds and norms of Muslims that started around the 18th century, is considered a significant reason for the change in attitude towards mental health (Ali-Faisal, 2020; Tunaboylu-İkiz, 1999). This is because psychological knowledge was utilised as a tool to 'civilise' Muslims. 'Modernisation' through Westernisation (i.e., importing Western ideas and approaches in medical, social, cultural, and other spheres of life/civilisation; Britannica, 2022) brought in a new understanding of health, illness,

DOI: 10.4324/9781003329589-1

and ideals of hospital systems, while a different framework for the diagnosis and treatment of mental illness took over (Haque, 2004). At the intersection of natural and social sciences, the mental health field became a unique and crucial arena within which imperialism and scientific knowledge interacted (Keller, 2001).

With the intention to excavate and reveal the incredible contributions of Islāmic heritage to the field of psychology, this book aims to provide the reader with an inspiring clinical model of the bīmaristāns (i.e., Islāmic hospitals, Latinised to maristān). We outline a blueprint for holistic psychiatric care once provided by the maristāns with the objective of reviving such a sophisticated tradition of mental health and healing in the modern world. This chapter provides an introduction to the terminology of the maristāns and offers a brief overview of the historical development of the early maristāns. The primary objective of this chapter is to demonstrate that the Islāmic worldview and traditions served as the motivation and inspiration behind the establishment of these advanced hospitals.

What Is a (Bī)Maristān?

Bīmaristān, or maristān for short, is composed of the Persian word '*Bīmār*' (illness) and the suffix '*-stān*' (place, house) and is synonymous with the word hospital today. With the spread of Islam came the geographical expansion of Muslim rule into new lands. Each of these expansions also brought about the construction of multiple trademark institutions such as *masājid* (houses of worship), *madāris* (schools for Islāmic learning), and maristāns (hospitals) to these new lands. The terms used to refer to the hospitals found in Muslim lands evolved over space and time. For example, the term *murustān* or *morstān* was commonly used in Egypt. *Mestrān* was more often encountered in the Maghreb region. In Islāmic Spain, the use of *malastān* or *marastān* and in Central Asia, the use of *dār al-marḍā* (i.e., 'home for the ill'; Terzioğlu, 1992) was the norm. During the Seljuk Dynasty and later in the Ottoman Empire, various terms were used synonymously, often composed of the word '*Dār*' (house, place) and an ending such as '*-Shifā'*' (healing), '*-Āfīyah*' (well-being), or '*-Ṣiḥḥa*' (health) or also '*Shifā' khana*', which is composed of '*Shifa*' and '*-khana*' (place/house; Benek et al., 2015). Table 1.1 summarises the different terminologies for Islāmic hospitals in different regions.

Despite some variation across regions and time periods, the spread of maristāns throughout Muslim lands led to the creation of a shared healing culture across time and space throughout Islāmic history. Hospitals established in later times—Ottoman dār al-shifā's, for instance—were built upon the pre-existing knowledge that was inherited from earlier Islāmic traditions, such as those of the Seljuks and the Abbasids (Altıntaş, 2022).

Table 1.1 Overview of different terms for maristāns by region

Term	*Translation*	*Region*
Bīmaristān/maristān	Place, house of/for the sick	Persia
Malastān/marastān	See bīmaristān	Spain
Murustān	See bīmaristān	Egypt
Morstān/mestrān	See bīmaristān	Maghreb
Dārulmerza	House for the sick	Central Asia
Dārulāfiye	Place/home of health	Near East/Anatolia
Dārüşşifā/dar al-shifa/darulshifa/ shifāhāne/darukhana	House of healing	Anatolia
Dār al-sıhha/sihat-khana	Home/house of health	Anatolia
Bīmārhāne/tımarhane/	House of/for the sick	Anatolia

The First Maristāns

Maristāns became a signature of the Islāmic civilisation by the 8th century. They could be found in every major metropolis across the Muslim world from the 10th century onwards, from the Iberian Peninsula to South Asia (Awaad et al., 2019). Typically, maristāns were either portable or fixed. Portable maristāns often arose from temporary demands caused by warfare or epidemics (Isa, 1939), whereas the fixed maristāns that constitute the subject of this book were established and operated as long-term institutions. Both types provided inpatient as well as outpatient medical care depending on the treatment requirements and the seriousness of the diagnoses.

Maristāns were built under the rule of each Muslim dynasty and offered medical care for physical ailments similar to hospitals of preceding and parallel civilisations (Sayılı, 1980). Their distinguishing mark, however, was the offering of medical treatment of psychiatric conditions that was noticeably absent from other hospitals. Beginning with the first known maristān established by Caliph al-Walīd ibn ʻAbd al-Malik ibn Marwān (d. 715 CE) in 706 CE, hospitals in Muslim lands were available and accessible to the mentally ill (Jetter, 1961; Mora, 2008). These medical institutions were established with exceptional diligence at the peak of Islāmic medicine, meaning that patients received the highest quality medical treatments and services available at the time (Awaad et al., 2019). These hospitals arguably resembled today's blue ribbon clinics in terms of advanced treatment, well-structured organisation, and proficient, interdisciplinary care teams (Hunke, 1965; Jetter, 1961).

For Context's Sake: Comparison to Institutionalised Mental Healthcare in Europe

The significance of offering psychiatric care in such an early period in human history becomes more apparent compared to the absence of such services in other medical cultures—specifically in Europe. There is a widespread assumption that the historical origins of psychotherapy lie with the Ancient Greeks, followed by a standstill until the 18th century when the 'birth of psychology' occurred in Europe. In today's clinical psychology and psychiatry training programmes, it is still taught that the works of the Ancient Greeks remained untouched for centuries (Schott & Tölle, 2006), and there were no advancements in the psychiatric or psychological fields until the 18th century (Shorter, 1998). Both these Eurocentric assumptions ignore the advancements in psychology by non-European civilisations.

Emerging research now clearly shows that the 9th and 10th centuries of the Islāmic civilisation were considered the heyday of psychotherapeutic orientation (Cohn & Farau, 1999), wherein client-centred approaches first appeared, providing the impetus for the development of psychotherapy (Slunecko, 2009). Despite the lack of acknowledgement in Western historical accounts, Dols (1992) describes in his book that 'the evidence for the medical care of the mentally ill in Islāmic hospitals before the 15th century is overwhelming' (p. 112). By comparison, as late as the 17th century in Europe, mental disorders were seen as the work and influence of the devil. As such, people with psychiatric illnesses were often persecuted as witches or sorcerers, often confined in wooden boxes or other custody houses (Schott & Tölle, 2006). This deplorable treatment of the mentally ill continued into the 18th century. German psychiatrist Emil Kraeplin (d. 1856 CE), to whom significant developments in scientific psychiatry are often attributed, describes that the condition of people with psychiatric illness throughout Europe at the turn of the 18th century was usually horrific (Kraepelin, 1918).

Furthermore, the beginning of institutionalised mental healthcare is typically marked in certain historical sources as the establishment of the Bethlem Royal Hospital in London in the 13th century, which is said to have admitted and housed individuals with mental disorders (MacDonald, 1981; Arnold, 2008), while other historians place the institutionalised treatment of mental health issues more prominently in 18th-century Europe (Le bonhomme & Le bras, 2021). A significant milestone in the development of psychiatric institutions occurred at the end of the 18th century when a psychiatric hospital in Vienna, 'Narrenturm' (i.e., Fool's Tower), was built around 1784 CE. The supposed innovativeness of this institution lay in the fact that contrary to the prevailing perspectives in Europe at the time, which conceptualised mental disorders as punishments from God, psychologically disturbed people were gradually seen as having a bona fide illness. Despite this shift, not much regarding the actual medical care itself had changed. Placing psychiatry patients in this sanatorium was more like locking them away rather than treating them for their conditions (Praschinger, 2010). Kraeplin describes the condition of the sick in these institutions in great detail in his early works:

> Corridors and wheezes are dark, in a manner resembling a dungeon in the highest degree, guarded by terribly massive iron doors and gates, rings, and

> bolts, so that certainly it would not be possible for the most refined criminal or villain to escape. The greatest uncleanliness, a hideous, unbearable stench, howling and roaring, a horrible, ghastly wailing of many, still on heavy chains and iron hoops, legs, and arms, even the necks of the most cruelly bound lunatics are objects that confront the visiting doctor in this tower. The poorest and most miserable of all the insane I have ever seen are kept and fed here like the wildest beasts of prey; the worst menagerie, however, still presents a far friendlier and more humane appearance. On all the faces and in the whole attitude of the lunatics, ghastly misery, pain, and despair are pronounced; on a meagre diet and under incessant pain of the body, caused by violent attempts at healing by means of perpetual vesicatories and the pustule ointment, these lamentable patients are not even granted what even the most serious criminals and murderers enjoy at least from time to time (...).
>
> Kraepelin (1918, p. 4)

Only in the years to follow did the treatment methods of mentally ill people in Europe steadily improve. Although there were similar observations from the same period in hospitals during the Ottoman Empire, which was by then in its decline (Akçura, 2023), this was not the norm for the preceding millennium in the Islāmic world. Instead, Islāmicate medicine, influenced by the traditions of ancient medicine that preceded it (Imamuddīn, 1978; Weisser, 1985) and inspired by Islāmic teachings that strongly emphasised the preservation of the intellect, was able to cultivate a rational, somatic view of people with mental disorders (Schott & Tölle, 2006). Since the advent of Islam, providing medical care to those suffering from psychiatric conditions has been observed as a *farḍ kifāyah* (communal obligation) on the entire society and the professional duty of Muslim physicians (Ibn Abidin, 1982). As such, it is imperative to point out that a major milestone undertaken by the Islāmic civilisation was instituting a dedicated psychiatric ward within a medical hospital that offered medicalised—not merely convalescent or spiritual—care for the mentally ill. As early as the 8th century, these psychiatric wards that were housed within maristāns from Islāmic antiquity were often characterised by their high-quality medical care, in addition to the clean, lavish accommodations provided during hospitalisation (Dols, 1992; Schipperges, 1962).

Insights into the structure, organisation, and treatment of the maristāns reveal the progressiveness and novelty with which mental illness was addressed in the Islāmic world. More importantly, the Eurocentric nature of the historiography of psychology as taught in universities and training programmes today needs rewriting, and credit for the advancements in the field should be appropriately attributed where due (Weiner, 2008).

An Islāmic Framework for Institutionalised Mental Healthcare

The framework for treating people with mental illness implemented in maristāns arose directly from the Islāmic religious tradition (Awaad et al.,

2019, 2020). The endowment and founding documents (see 'Unveiling the Motivations for the Establishment of the Maristāns') and others like them found throughout Islāmic history make it very clear that the treatment many patients received at maristāns across the Islāmic world was often inspired and motivated by Islāmic principles.

Islāmically, health is a top priority because any obstacle that hinders a person's ability to worship God is one that requires immediate attention (Al-Qarafi, 1973). Schipperges (2003) notes that Islam is the only major world religion to have the root of the word 'health' in its name and has thus made the concept of well-being a foundation of its worldview. The root letters of the word Islam (م[*mīm*],ل[*lām*],س[*sīn*]) can be understood as the all-round well-being of body, soul, and mind (Schipperges, 2003).

In order to understand the Islāmic framework for institutionalised mental healthcare, it is essential to understand the three sources from which the Islāmic religious tradition originates:

1 Qur'ān: the holy book in Islam, the word of Allāh (God, ﷻ) that was revealed to Prophet Muḥammad (ﷺ, d. 632 CE).
2 Ḥadīth and Sunnah of Prophet Muḥammad (ﷺ), which includes the sayings, actions, and tacit approvals of the Messenger (ﷺ).
3 *Ijmā'* and *Qiyās*, which are not independent sources but are derived from the Qur'ān and the Sunnah. While *Ijmā'* is the consensus of Islāmic legal scholars, *Qiyās* in Islāmic jurisprudence is a form of analogical deduction that can be applied as a means of finding norms on a particular issue when there is no ruling mentioned in the Qur'ān or Sunnah nor a scholarly consensus on it.

In these sources, numerous references and instructions likely shaped the establishment of these institutions, particularly the humane treatment of the mentally ill. The following section will outline how these sources provided the impetus and motivation for the humane treatment of people with mental illness and the construction of hospitals to help care for them.

Mental Health in the Qur'ān and Sunnah

The Qur'ān has significantly changed people's understanding and attitude towards illness and diseases. Contrary to the Medieval Christian assumption that illness is a punishment from God for one's sins (Dols, 1992), specifically the original sin, Islam teaches that God will test people with their health and well-being and reward them for their patience: 'And We will surely test you with something of fear and hunger and a loss of wealth and lives and fruits, but give glad tidings to the patient' (*The Qur'ān*, 2:155). This approach to diseases completely differs from explanatory models of illness in other faiths. Even the prophets, the most outstanding servants of Allāh (ﷻ), were subjected to various trials regarding their health. In this respect, Prophet Ayyub's patience, fortitude, and trustworthiness in the face of severe illnesses are some of the most critical and meaningful examples for Muslims. Also, the verse 'There is not upon the blind [any] constraint nor upon the lame constraint nor upon the ill constraint…' (*The Qur'ān*, 24:61) changed the common understanding towards people who fall ill. The famous scholar Imam al-Qurṭubī (d. 1273 CE) narrates the following about the commentary (i.e., Tafsīr) of the mentioned verse:

> Before the Prophet Muḥammad (ﷺ) was sent, the Arabs and those in Madina used to abstain from eating with those who were afflicted with various diseases. Some of them were disgusted by the fact that a blind person's hand would touch random places, or a lame person would sit in a random way, or a sick person would smell and be uncomfortable, so they would avoid eating with such people, but this is an ignorant morality and arrogance. This verse was revealed as a warning in this regard.
>
> Al-Qurṭubī (2001, p. 482)

Another verse that shaped and changed the attitudes towards the needy is:

> And do not give the weak-minded your property, which Allāh (ﷻ) has made a means of sustenance for you, but provide for them with it and clothe them and speak to them words of appropriate kindness.
>
> The Qur'ān (4:5)

It is these verses that the early Muslims took to heart and possibly inspired their humane treatment of the mentally ill, which was reflected in the building of the maristāns and the treatment of their patients. In addition to these Qur'ānic verses, the Prophet Muḥammad (ﷺ) also contributed to changing attitudes towards diseases. The Prophet (ﷺ), who, according to the Qur'ān, does not speak from his own inclination (*The Qur'ān*, 53:3), says in a Ḥadīth, 'There is no disease that Allāh (ﷻ) has created, except that He also has created its treatment' (Al-Bukhârî) and 'Make use of medical treatment, for Allāh (ﷻ) has not made a disease without appointing a remedy for it, with the exception of one condition, namely old age' (Abū Dāwūd, 3855). Taken together with the condemnation of magic and similar practices in the Qur'ān (Dols, 1992), these expressions of the Prophet (ﷺ) led Muslims away from seeking occultist salvation and instead towards seeking treatment and medicine (Çetin, 2012). As part of the Prophet Muḥammad's (ﷺ) morning supplications, he would say: 'O Allāh! I seek refuge in You from worry and grief…'. Likewise, the Prophet (ﷺ) used to say: 'O Allāh, I seek refuge in You from leprosy, madness, elephantiasis, and the worst diseases' (Abū Dāwūd, 1554). The fact that the Prophet (ﷺ) sought refuge in Allāh (ﷻ) from psychological problems and other severe diseases in his daily prayers can be seen as an indication that this subject was important and addressed during the Prophet's (ﷺ) lifetime.

One other Islāmic principle influential in the Islāmic dedication to mental healthcare possibly stems from the fact that the Prophet (ﷺ) defines visiting the sick as one of the rights of a Muslim upon a fellow Muslim (Muslim, 2162). The essence of visiting and caring for the sick is grounded in the Islāmic belief that Allāh (ﷻ) will be merciful in the hereafter to the one who is merciful to people on earth (Çınar, 2017). This basic Islāmic assumption towards people with diseases and the care towards them, and the resulting benefits from Allāh (ﷻ), becomes very clear once again in the following Saḥīḥ Ḥadīth:

> Verily, Allāh, the Exalted and Glorious, would say on the Day of Resurrection: 'O son of Adam, I was sick, but you did not visit Me.' He would say: 'O my Lord; how could I visit You whereas You are the Lord of the worlds?' Thereupon, He would say: 'Didn't you know that such and such servant of Mine was sick, but you did not visit him, and were you not aware of this that if you had visited him, you would have found Me by him?
>
> Muslim (2569)

Further, the Prophet (ﷺ) taught excellence in character (Al-Adab al-Mufrad, 273), emotional honesty, and connection (Abū Dāwūd, 3126; 4969), and the theological framework that no believer is ever 'stricken with discomfort, hardship, or illness, grief, or even a mental worry' except that he is expiated in return (Saḥīḥ Muslim, 2573). From an Islāmic perspective, illnesses are not a reason for the isolation of sick people but, rather, a cause for support from social contacts and even the general Muslim public. From the historical records of the maristāns, it is known that the hospitals were very consciously built in a central location in the city to be more easily accessible to people (Awaad et al., 2019; Ragab, 2015). This inclusive attitude also enabled the mentally ill to be treated, while remaining a part of their society and allowing relatives to visit them more easily (Lev, 2005). In addition to historical records mentioning that relatives were permitted to visit patients in the maristāns (Dols, 1992), the existence of waiting rooms for visitors, such as in the maristān in al-Qayrawan (Terzioğlu, 1992), is another important indicator that confirms the validity of this supposition.

Mental Health in Islāmic Legal Texts

According to Muslim scholars, the *'aql* (intellect) is the greatest blessing given to humankind (Al-Dhahabi, 1981). It is described as a structure that allows humans to distinguish the beautiful from the ugly, the distorted from the straight, to analyse events, and to make judgements. More succinctly, having *'aql* is having a mind (Çınar, 2017). In addition, the intellect provides reason and puts human beings under obligations and responsibilities in the presence of divine commands (Bolay, 1989). A person's religious practices consist of commandments, prohibitions, and responsibilities to oneself, one's family, and one's society. Questions regarding these responsibilities are clarified in the Islāmic fiqh (legal discipline). According to Islāmic law, whether a person is considered to have full capacity depends on whether mental disability hinders the person's ability to differentiate wrong from right (Dönmez, 1993). If so, it is called *junūn* (madness or mental impairment; Ali & Keshavarzi, 2017). People with *junūn* are exempted from certain religious practices due to their lack of discernment. The Prophet's (ﷺ) saying, 'Three persons are released from responsibility: The child until they reach the age of puberty, the sleeper until they wake up, and the *majnūn/ma'tūh* (one who is mad or mentally ill) until they are cured' (Tirmidhî, 1423) guides these regulations in the Islāmic legal context. In addition, two points in this Ḥadīth are worth mentioning. First, the mention of mental impairment by the Prophet (ﷺ) can be considered as evidence that this topic was present even during his lifetime. On the other hand, the expression 'until he is cured' implies the understanding of mental illnesses as diseases with existing treatments.

Furthermore, the 'preservation of the intellect/mental faculties' is considered one of the five main objectives of Islāmic legislation in general because the principle is that everything that is required to fulfil a duty becomes itself a duty (Al-Qarafi, 1973). In light of this, the importance of a person's mental health in Islam is further elucidated. The establishment of institutions for individuals with mental illness can be understood within the Islāmic injunction of eliminating dangers to one's physical and mental well-being through preventive measures (Ibn Nujaym, 1983).

Thus, sound mental health is the prerequisite for a person to understand the divine message, align one's life with it, and perform obligatory religious practices. What is evident from the accounts mentioned earlier is that sound mental health is one of the key ingredients for Muslims to attain the pleasure of Allāh (ﷻ) and enjoy a state of well-being in this world and in the hereafter.

Eliminating the Weeds: Differentiating the Cultural from the Religious

One noteworthy challenge in establishing an Islāmic foundation for the clinical practice of IP is to ensure that the 'Islāmic' aspect of IP is sound Islāmically. It is essential to source Islāmic elements directly from the Qur'ān, Ḥadīth, and the relied-upon sources of the classical Islāmic tradition that are rooted in the Qur'ān and Sunnah. Hence, a crucial distinction would be to distinguish between what is Islāmic in its origin versus what a Muslim person may have theorised. This means that an idea or practice deduced by a Muslim does not necessarily mean it will be sound

Islāmically. Furthermore, there is a wide variation in what the term 'Islāmic' incorporates (Keshavarzi et al., 2020). This distinction is necessary not only to filter through scholarship produced by Muslims historically, but is also essential in screening modern psychology scholarship for Islāmic appropriateness. For instance, ibn Sīnā was considered a genius in medicine whose ideas were influential beyond his time and well through the 16th century in both the Muslim lands and Europe (Awaad et al., 2020). However, scholars of Islāmic theology highly criticised his controversial stance on Islāmic metaphysics/theology (e.g., emergence theory) as a divergence from traditional Sunni principles of Islam. As such, we would refer to ibn Sīnā as a Muslim scholar and not an Islāmic scholar. In this context, it is crucial to differentiate between ibn Sīnā's medical contributions versus his contentious ideas on metaphysics in trying to assess which of his ideas may be safely incorporated into the current practice of IP.

Another essential aspect to consider in differentiating the 'Islāmic' element in the field of IP are the cultural norms that infiltrate into the thinking and practice of Muslims throughout history. Cultural practices in history can readily be interpreted as Islāmic because they were part of the practices of earlier Muslim societies. However, just as the dominant culture mixes with the Islāmic lifestyle (e.g., 'Islāmic' mindfulness) today, the ethnic or cultural elements that existed historically may be hard to distinguish from the Islāmic influence of how Muslims lived in the past. For example, shamanism (i.e., an indigenous religion that was practised by some Turkish tribes in Central Asia) was known to find its way from the Central Asian past of the Turks into the folkloric Turkish-Islāmic medical tradition (Shefer-Mossensohn, 2009). These pre-Islāmic elements included mystical healing practices mixed with other healing cultures, in some cases with Sufi practices, which existed in parallel with the mainstream medical practices that were popular during the Seljuk and Ottoman empires. As such, care must be taken to ensure that practices commonly used by Muslims have an Islāmic basis and are not merely part of popular culture.

Unveiling the Motivations for the Establishment of the Maristāns

As we have discussed, hospitals held an important place in Islāmic civilisations. They were often approached with the same care as *masājid* (mosques) and *madāris* (literally, places of study) and were frequently established or supported by the rulers of their times. Upon the charitable establishment of such hospitals, each patron/sponsor would compose an official waqf [1] document that listed their reasons and motivations for the endowment, its rules, means, and restrictions of usage and their expectations for how the hospital would benefit others. An examination of these institutions' waqf documents reveals the extent to which the Islāmic sources of inspiration and motivation related to mental health, as described in the previous sections, were decisive in the founding and upkeep of these institutions.

Because sponsoring the building of hospitals was a reliable means of fulfilling the Islāmic obligation of charity to the disadvantaged, maristāns were supported generously by sultans, other high-ranking bureaucrats, and wealthy families (Dols, 1987, 1992). This is evident, for example, from the waqf document of Bīmaristān al-Qalāwūn, where it was instructed that medical treatment in this maristān was to be made available to everyone in need, free of charge (Isa, 1939).

A visitor to a maristān in Baghdad described the following:

> I also visited a palace there called Dar al-Marhama, which means House of Mercy. In it, all the insane people of the whole area stay in closed compartments or under a cure. [...] This was established by the authorities for motives of mercy and for purposes of charity. It is generally intended to benefit those suffering from insanity and the like.
>
> Schipperges (1962)

Indeed, establishing a hospital to care for the ill is part of the Islāmic concept of *ṣadaqah jāriyah*, which is an ongoing, permanent act of charity that retains its power to benefit both the beneficiaries and the donor even after the donor passes away (Duman, 2008). This is in accordance with the Prophet's (ﷺ) saying: 'When a person dies, the rewards of all their deeds are cut off except these three: *ṣadaqah jāriyah*, the knowledge that is benefited from, and good children who pray for them after [they have passed]' (Tirmidhî, 1376). Islāmic scholars have often stated that *ṣadaqah jāriyah* is already implied when one sets up a waqf (Elasrag, 2017). In his commentary on this Ḥadīth, Imam Nawawi (d. 1277) describes that the *ṣadaqah jāriyah* is the waqf itself (Al-Nawawi, 1994). According to another approach, since the waqf itself is a *ṣadaqah*, it is defined as an act of *birr* (giving charity out of goodness) (Ahmed, 2007). This type of Islāmic charitable motivation can be seen in the deed of the maristān of Ibrahim ibn Naṣr. Ibn Naṣr established a maristān in 1066 CE in Samarkand, Uzbekistan, as a sign of gratitude to God for achieving prosperity and victory over his enemies (Lev, 2005). This act of *ṣadaqah* upon victory is derived from the Qur'ān (9:75): 'And among them are those who made a covenant with Allāh (ﷻ), [saying], "If He should give us from His bounty, we will surely spend in charity, and we will surely be among the righteous"' (Ansari, 2013).

Another act of *ṣadaqah* is found in the waqf documents of Bīmaristān al-Fariki, considered one of Anatolia's oldest Islāmic hospitals. It is believed that this maristān was built during the Marwanid era (983–1085 CE) under the direction of Amir Nāṣir al-Dawla (1011–1061 CE). According to ibn Abī Uṣaybi'ah, the hospital was established after Nāṣir al-Dawla made a personal commitment as an Islāmic vow to donate an amount equivalent to the weight of his ailing daughter should she recover. After the physician Zahid al-Ulemā (d. 1042 CE) successfully treated the daughter, he suggested that Nāṣir al-Dawla (r. 1011–1061 CE) use the money as a donation to build a hospital. He accepted this proposal and proceeded to establish a hospital, for which he also contributed assets (Acıduman & Tuzcu, 2016).

Among the hospitals that emerged throughout the Islāmic world, one of the most prominent ones was built in Cairo by the Egyptian Sultan al-Manṣūr Saif al-Din Qalāwūn (d.1290). The widespread view is that when Sultan Qalāwūn was still a prince, he suffered from severe colic, and the doctors healed him with medicines from Maristān Nūr al-Dīn. Subsequently, al-Manṣūr himself visited the maristān, was amazed by it, and vowed to God that if he ever became Sultan, he would build such a hospital himself (Dols, 1992; Hunke, 1965; Isa, 1939). Eventually, Sultan al-Manṣūr established the Qalāwūn Bīmaristān. Relevant passages of the waqf deed that he provided for the hospital are presented below with a meaning-based translation. It clarifies the intention and purpose with which this maristān was founded:

> (Line 42–44) It is no secret that it is good deeds that give relief to a needy patient, bring joy to the broken heart, and make it rich by sheltering and treating it. Blessed are they who work for their Lord (...)
>
> (Line 47–50) That person who helps the poor Muslim by relieving his pain and healing his illness. Through this help, he will be saved from the punishment of his Creator tomorrow. **And he does this act in the hopes of attaining a high rank in the sight of Allāh, and in the hopes of nearness to Allāh on the Day of Judgment because of the reward of his good deeds**, and in the hopes of achieving good deeds that will not leave any sin/evil.
>
> (Line 51/83) When Sultan Malik Manṣūr understood this (...), he gave the command (...)
>
> (Line 296) Different treatments (shall be offered in this Maristān) according to the type or nature of the wound (...) whether they are physical (more or less) (...) and the diseases of the intellect—**since the preservation of the intellect is the most important aspect/goal.**

Finally, the following section of the waqf deed confirms that the maristān was established with the intention of *ṣadaqah jāriyah*:

> (Line 328–330): All these efforts are made in the hope that Sultan Malik Manṣūr will be accepted by his Lord. Indeed, the Messenger of Allāh says in a Saḥīḥ Ḥadīth: When a person dies, the rewards of all their deeds are cut off except these three: *ṣadaqah jāriyah*, knowledge that is benefited from, and good children who pray for them after [they have died].

The waqf documents quoted above emphasise the importance of the maristān to be beneficial to people, to be a balm to their wounds, to espouse compassionate care, and to approach people mercifully, all per Islāmic teachings.

A good deed done for a sick person is a good deed done for Allāh (ﷻ), and preserving the mind was considered the most important goal.

Conclusion

Maristāns, as Islāmically inspired hospitals that served patients for centuries, addressed the physical and psychological treatment of diseases and took a holistic approach to patient care. They recognised that physical, mental, and spiritual well-being are closely linked and interrelated. This holistic approach, practised within the maristāns, meant going beyond the treatment of symptoms to consider the overall well-being and dignity of the individual. It means looking at patients not just as medical cases but as complex human beings with unique needs. The exploration and elaborations on historical sources reveal a profound connection between the establishment of maristāns; the advanced treatment approaches practised within them; and the motivations for their establishment that were often rooted in Islāmic principles. Furthermore, endowment documents not only clarify the commitment to the mentally ill stemming directly from Islāmic sources but also speak to the moral standards of the medieval and pre-modern Muslim society in which founders, physicians, and staff felt an obligation and responsibility towards the patients with mental illness regardless of origin, religion, or wealth and provided them with excellent care.

Note

1 *Waqf* refers to a Muslim's permanent dedication of property for charitable, religious, or specific personal purposes. This dedication extinguishes the donor's rights to the property, ensuring the property serves the defined objectives during their lifetime and after, often extending to their descendants or a purpose chosen by the founder (Peters et al., 2012).

References

Abū Dāwūd, S. (n.d.). *A man should seek a remedy*. sunnah.com – Sayings and teachings of Prophet Muḥammad (ﷺ). https://sunnah.com/abudawud:3855

Abū Dāwūd, S. (n.d.). *General Behavior*. sunnah.com – Sayings and teachings of Prophet Muḥammad (ﷺ). https://sunnah.com/abudawud:4969

Abū Dāwūd, S. (n.d.). *Regarding Seeking Refuge*. sunnah.com – Sayings and teachings of Prophet Muḥammad (ﷺ). https://sunnah.com/abudawud:1554

Abū Dāwūd, S. (n.d.). *Weeping for the Deceased*. sunnah.com – Sayings and teachings of Prophet Muḥammad (ﷺ). https://sunnah.com/abudawud:3126

Acıduman, A., & Tuzcu, K. (2016). Meyyâfârikîn Bîmâristânı Üzerine Bazı Yeni BilgilerIşığında Bir Değerlendirme. *Belleten*, *80*(289), 741–756. https://doi.org/10.37879/belleten.2016.741

Ahmed, H. (2007). *Waqf-based Microfinance: Realizing the Social Role of Islāmic Finance*. World Bank.

Akçura, Y. (2023). *Osmanlı Devleti'nin Dağılma Devri*. Ötüken Neşriyat.

Al-Bukhârî, M. (n.d.). *Good Conduct*. sunnah.com – Sayings and teachings of Prophet Muḥammad (ﷺ). https://sunnah.com/adab:237

Al-Bukhârî, M. (n.d.). *There is no disease except its treatment*. sunnah.com – Sayings and teachings of Prophet Muḥammad (ﷺ). https://sunnah.com/bukhari:5678

Al-Bukhârî, M. (n.d.). *What has been mentioned about the plague*. sunnah.com – Sayings and teachings of Prophet Muḥammad (ﷺ). https://sunnah.com/bukhari:5728

Al-Dhahabi. (1981). *Siyar A'lām al-Nubalā': Vol. 8*. https://archive.org/details/FP11950/san08/page/n395/mode/2up?view=theater

Ali, B., & Keshavarzi, H. (2017, Oct 30). Forensic psychiatry. In *Oxford Islamic Studies*. https://www.oxfordislamicstudies.com/article/opr/t343/e0250

Ali-Faisal, S. F. (2020). Islamic anti-patriarchal liberation psychology: A framework to decolonise psychology for Muslims. *Feminism & Psychology*, *30*(3), 343–362. https://doi.org/10.1177/0959353520941350

Al-Karam, C. Y. (2018). Islamic psychology: Towards a 21st century definition and conceptual framework. *Journal of Islamic Ethics*, *2*(1–2), 97–109. https://doi.org/10.1163/24685542-12340020

Al-Nasā'i, A. (n.d.). *The Virtue of Charity Given on Behalf of the Deceased*. sunnah.com – Sayings and teachings of Prophet Muḥammad (ﷺ). https://sunnah.com/nasai:3651

Al-Nawawi, I. M. (1994). *Sahih Muslim bi sharh al-Imam Muhyi al-Din Yahya ibn Sharaf al-musamma al-Minhaj sharh Sahih Muslim ibn al-Hajjaj*. Dar al-Ma'rifa.

Al-Qarafi (1973). *AI Sharh Tanqih al-Fusul*. Technical Printing United Company.

Al-Qurṭubī, M. A. (2001). *El-Câmiʿ li-aḥkâmi'l-Ḳur'ân ve'l-mübeyyin limâ teżammenehû mine's-sünneti ve âyi'l-furḳān': Vol. 12*. Buruc Yayinlari. https://archive.org/details/ImamKurtubiTefsiriElCamiuLiAhkamilKuran2

Altıntaş, A. (2022). Anadolu Tibbi Nedir-Neden Önemlidir? *Anadolu Tıbbı Dergisi*, *1*(1), *1*.

Al-Tirmidhî, M. (n.d.). *What has been related about a Waqf*. sunnah.com – sayings and teachings of Prophet Muḥammad (ﷺ). https://sunnah.com/tirmidhi:1376

Al-Tirmidhî, M. (n.d.). *What has been related about those from whom punishment is not required*. sunnah.com – Sayings and teachings of Prophet Muḥammad (ﷺ). https://sunnah.com/tirmidhi:1423

Ansari, M. A. (2013). *Bīmāristāns and Waqf In Islam: Case Studies of Hospital Endowment during the 9th to 13th Century CE in the Muslim World*. https://www.academia.edu/6955050

Arnold, C. (2008). *Bedlam: London, and Its Mad*. Simon & Schuster.

Awaad, R., Elsayed, D., Ali, S., & Abid, A. (2020). Islamic psychology: A portrait of its historical origins and Contributions. In *Applying Islamic Principles to Clinical Mental Health Care*. Routledge.

Awaad, R., Mohammad, A., Elzamzamy, K., Fereydooni, S., & Gamar, M. (2019). Mental health in the Islamic golden era: The historical roots of modern psychiatry. In H. S. Moffic, J. Peteet, A. Z. Hankir, & R. Awaad (Eds.), *Islamophobia and Psychiatry: Recognition, Prevention, and Treatment* (pp. 3–17). Springer. https://doi.org/10.1007/978-3-030-00512-2_1

Benek, B., Sakar, H., Bayram, R., & Gumustekin, K. (2015). The oldest medical center of the anatolia: Gevher nesibe darussifa and medical school. *Acta Medica Anatolia*, *3*, 108. https://www.researchgate.net/publication/283276209_

The_Oldest_Medical_Center_of_the_Anatolia_Gevher_Nesibe_Darussifa_and_Medical_School

Bolay, S. H. (1989). AKIL. *TDV İslâm Ansiklopedisi*. https://islamansiklopedisi.org.tr/akil

Britannica. (2022). The editors of encyclopaedia: Westernization. *Encyclopedia Britannica*, 14 February 2022. https://www-britannica-com.stanford.idm.oclc.org/topic/Westernization

Çapan, F. (2019). İslam Dünyası'nda Bimaristanlar ve Gelişme Süreçleri. *Gaziantep University Journal of Social Sciences*, *18*, 1205–1219. https://doi.org/10.21547/jss.492008

Çetin, O. (2012). Sifahanelerin Manevi Temelleri, Anadolu ve Osmanl Sefkat Abideleri Sifahanele. In A. Kiliç (Ed.), *Diasan Basim* (pp. 62–64). Diasan Basım.

Çınar, H. İ. (2017). *Gönül Yazıları*. IFIS&IZ Publications.

Cohn, R. C., & Farau, A. (1999). Gelebte Geschichte der Psychotherapie. *Klett-Cotta*. https://www.lehmanns.de/shop/geisteswissenschaften/2403045-9783608941784-gelebte-geschichte-der-psychotherapie-konzepte-der-humanwissenschaften

Dols, M. W. (1987). The origins of the Islamic hospital: Myth and reality. *Bulletin of the History of Medicine*, *61*(3), 367–390.

Dols, M. W. (1992). *Majnūn: The madman in medieval Islamic Society*. https://doi.org/10.1093/acprof:oso/9780198202219.001.0001

Dönmez, I. K. (1993). CÜNÛN. *TDV İslâm Ansiklopedisi*. https://islamansiklopedisi.org.tr/cunun

Duman, A. (2008). SADAKA. *TDV İslâm Ansiklopedisi*. https://islamansiklopedisi.org.tr/sadaka

Elasrag, H. (2017). *Towards a New Role of the Institution of Waqf*. Social Science Research Network. https://doi.org/10.2139/ssrn.3011290

Elkassem, S., Csiernik, R., Mantulak, A. et al. (2018). Growing up Muslim: The impact of islamophobia on children in a Canadian community. *Journal of Muslim Mental Health*, *12* (1). pp. 3–18. ISSN 1556–4908

Haque, A. (2004). Psychology from Islamic perspective: Contributions of early Muslim scholars and challenges to contemporary Muslim psychologists. *Journal of Religion and Health*, *43*, 357–377. https://doi.org/10.1007/s10943-004-4302-z

Hunke, S. (1965). Allāhs Sonne über dem Abendland: Unser arabisches Erbe (65; Von d. Autorin bearb. Ausg). *Fischer Bücherei*. https://menadoc.bibliothek.uni-halle.de/inhouse-vgg/content/titleinfo/4896312

Ibn Abidin. (1982). *Reddü'l Muhtar Ale'd Dürri'l-Muhtar*. Şamil Yay.

Ibn al-Hajjaj, M. (n.d.). *The Book of Greetings*. sunnah.com - sayings and teachings of Prophet Muḥammad (ﷺ). https://sunnah.com/muslim:2162a

Ibn al-Hajjaj, M. (n.d.). *The Reward of the Believer for Whatever Befalls Him of Sickness, Grief and the Like, Even A Thorn that Pricks Him*. sunnah.com - sayings and teachings of Prophet Muḥammad (ﷺ). https://sunnah.com/muslim:2573

Ibn al-Hajjaj, M. (n.d.). *The Virtue of Visiting the Sick*. sunnah.com - sayings and teachings of Prophet Muḥammad (ﷺ). https://sunnah.com/muslim:2569

Ibn Nujaym. (1983). al-Ashbah wa-al-naza'ir. *Dar al-Fikr, Beirut*.

Imamuddīn, S. M. (1978). Māristān (hospitals) in medieval Spain. *Islamic Studies*, *17*(1), 45–55

Isa, A. (1939). *Tārīkh Al-Bīmāristānāt Fī Al-Islām*. Jamiyyat al-Taḍāmun al-Islāmī.

Isgandarova, N. (2019). Muraqaba as a mindfulness-based therapy in Islamic psychotherapy. *Journal of Religion and Health*, *58*(4), 1146–1160 https://doi.org/10.1007/s10943-018-0695-y

Jetter, D. (1961). Zur Architektur islamischer Krankenhäuser. *Sudhoffs Archiv Für Geschichte Der Medizin Und Der Naturwissenschaften*, *45*(3), 261–273.

Kaplick, P. M., & Skinner, R. (2017). The evolving Islam and psychology movement. *European Psychologist*, *22*(3), 198–204. https://doi.org/10.1027/1016-9040/a000297

Keller, R. (2001). Madness and colonization: Psychiatry in the British and French empires, 1800–1962. *Journal of Social History*, *35*(2), 295–326. https://www.jstor.org/stable/3790190

Keshavarzi, H., & Ali, B. (2019). Islamic perspectives on psychological and spiritual well-being and treatment. In H. S. Moffic, J. Peteet, A. Z. Hankir, & R. Awaad (Eds.), *Islamophobia and Psychiatry: Recognition, Prevention, and Treatment* (pp. 41–53). Springer. https://doi.org/10.1007/978-3-030-00512-2_4

Keshavarzi, H., & Haque, A. (2013). Outlining a psychotherapy model for enhancing Muslim mental health within an Islamic context. *The International Journal for the Psychology of Religion*, *23*(3), 230–249. https://doi.org/10.1080/10508619.2012.712000

Keshavarzi, H., Khan, F., Ali, B., & Awaad, R. (2020). *Applying Islamic Principles to Clinical Mental Health Care: Introducing Traditional Islamically Integrated Psychotherapy*. Routledge.

Kraepelin, E. (1918). *Hundert Jahre Psychiatrie: Ein Beitrag zur Geschichte menschlicher Gesittung*. Springer.

Le bonhomme, F. & Le bras, A. (2021). Psychiatric institutions in Europe, nineteenth and twentieth century. *Encyclopédie d'histoire numérique de l'Europe*. https://ehne.fr/en/node/14132

Lev, Y. (2005). *Charity, Endowments, and Charitable Institutions in Medieval Islam*. University Press of Florida.

MacDonald, M. (1981). *Mystical Bedlam: Madness, Anxiety and Healing in Seventeenth-Century England*. Cambridge University Press

Mora, G. (2008). Mental disturbances, unusual mental states, and their interpretation during the Middle Ages. In Wallace, E. & Gach, J. (Eds.) *History of Psychiatry and Medical Psychology: With an Epilogue on Psychiatry and the Mind-Body Relation* (pp. 199–226). Springer.

Praschinger, A. (2010). Der Wiener Narrenturm. *Psychopraxis*, *13*(5), 14–17. https://doi.org/10.1007/s00739-010-0247-z

Ragab, A. (2015). *The Medieval Islamic Hospital: Medicine, Religion, and Charity* (1st ed.). Cambridge University Press. https://doi.org/10.1017/CBO9781316271797

Rassool, G. H. (2021). *Islamic Psychology: Human Behaviour and Experience from an Islamic Perspective* (1st ed.). Routledge. https://doi.org/10.4324/9780429354762

Rothman, A., & Coyle, A. (2018). Toward a framework for Islamic psychology and psychotherapy: An Islamic model of the soul. *Journal of Religion and Health*, *57*(5), 1731–1744. https://doi.org/10.1007/s10943-018-0651-x

Saheeh International. (n.d.). *English Translation of the Meaning of the Holy Qur'ān*. Conveying Islāmic Message Society.

Sayılı, A. (1980). The emergence of the prototype of the modern hospital in medieval Islam. *Belleten*, *44*(174), 279–286.

Schipperges, H. (1962). Einflüsse arabischer Medizin auf die Mikrokosmosliteratur des 12. Jahrhunderts. In P. Wilpert (Ed.), *Antike und Orient im Mittelalter.* De Gruyter. https://doi.org/10.1515/9783111342108.129

Schipperges, H. (2003). Das Mittelalter. In: *Gesundheit und Gesellschaft. Schriften der Mathematisch-naturwissenschaftlichen Klasse der Heidelberger Akademie der Wissenschaften*: *Vol: 12*. Springer. https://doi.org/10.1007/978-3-642-55479-7_4

Schott, H., & Tölle, R. (2006). *Geschichte der Psychiatrie: Krankheitslehren, Irrwege, Behandlungsformen*. C.H.Beck.

Şentürk, R. (2020). *Comparative Theories and Methods : Between Uniplexity and Multiplexity* (1st ed.). İbn Haldun University Press.

Shefer-Mossensohnm, M.(2009). *Ottoman Medicine: Healing and Medical Institutions, 1500–1700.* State University of New York Press.

Shoib, S., Gaitán Buitrago, J. E. T., Shuja, K. H., Aqeel, M., de Filippis, R., Abbas, J., Ullah, I., & Arafat, S. M. Y. (2022). Suicidal behavior sociocultural factors in developing countries during COVID-19. *L'Encéphale*, *48*(1), 78–82, https://doi.org/10.1016/j.encep.2021.06.011.

Shorter, E. (1998). *A History of Psychiatry: From the Era of the Asylum to the Age of Prozac*. Wiley.

Slunecko, T. (Ed.). (2009). *Psychotherapie: Eine Einführung* (1. Aufl). Facultas. Wuv.

Terzioğlu, A. (1992). Bîmâristan. İn *TDV İslâm Araştırmaları Merkezi.* https://islamansiklopedisi.org.tr/bimaristan

Tunaboylu-İkiz, T. (1999). Türk psikiyatri tarihi ve psikanalizin yeri. *Psikoloji Çalışmaları*, *21*, 159–168.

Weiner, D. B. (2008). The madman in the light of reason. Enlightenment psychiatry: Part II. Alienists, Treatises, and the psychologic approach in the era of Pinel. In Wallace, E.R., Gach, J. (eds) *History of Psychiatry and Medical Psychology: With an Epilogue on Psychiatry and the Mind-Body Relation* (pp. 281–303). Springer.

Weisser, U. (1985). Zwischen Antike und europäischem Mittelalter Die arabisch-islamische Medizin in ihrer klassischen Epoche. *Medizinhistorisches Journal*, *20*(4), 319–341.

World Health Organization. (2021). Mental Health ATLAS 2020. World Health Organization. https://iris.who.int/bitstream/handle/10665/345946/9789240036703-eng.pdf?sequence=1

2 The Formation of Maristāns across Time and Space

Rayan Ahmed Ansari and Merve Nursoy-Demir

Introduction

In the Islāmic world, maristāns rose not only as essential healthcare institutions but also as pillars of medical innovation and education, defining the landscape of Islāmic societies. Despite spanning diverse geographical regions and persisting across centuries, maristāns were remarkably consistent in their trademark features, motivations, foundations, and operation. This uniformity from Central Asia to the Iberian Peninsula underscores the importance of maristāns as a hallmark of the Islāmic civilisation (McClary, 2021).

By exploring various maristāns, each unique in its geographical and temporal context, we uncover a collective embodiment of the fundamental Islāmic principles that are inherent to all of these institutions. While the diversity of maristān founders—ranging from princesses to freed slaves[1]—is vast, these founders consistently demonstrate an Islāmically inspired motivation to establish these institutions. By examining a subset of fourteen maristāns, this chapter sheds light on their shared characteristics, illustrating how they collectively symbolise a pivotal aspect of Islāmic civilisation, transcending variations in rulers, regions, and historical periods. In this chapter, it should be noted that we use 'maristān', 'bīmaristān', and other regional terminologies interchangeably, reflecting the specific nomenclatures used historically and to both honour and celebrate the linguistic and cultural diversity that is encompassed by this healthcare institution.

A Snapshot of Maristāns through Time and Space

The Levant and Egypt

Al-Fusṭāṭ/Ibn Ṭūlūn Hospital (Est. 872 CE)

Aḥmad ibn Ṭūlūn (d. 884 CE), initially a former slave soldier within the Abbasid Caliphate, ascended the ranks to establish himself as an independent ruler. He founded the Ṭūlūnid dynasty and ruled Egypt and Syria from

DOI: 10.4324/9781003329589-2

868 to 884 CE (Hassan, 2012). Leveraging the economic prosperity of the time under his rule, Ibn Ṭūlūn constructed Egypt's first maristāns in 872–874 (Savage-Smith, 1994). Located in al-Fusṭāṭ, a predominantly military city, the maristān had a clear mission: to provide care for the poor, sick, and needy. The Sultan's decree explicitly emphasised that it was not intended for his high-ranking soldiers, highlighting its role as a genuine gift to the broader community rather than a military facility that incidentally served the public (Corbet, 1891).

The maristān had a substantial endowment valued at 60,000 dinars (roughly $5,000,000 in today's currency) and featured separate divisions for both sexes, designated baths for men and women, and specialised wards for specific illnesses or procedures (Corbet, 1891; Ragab, 2015). Patients received new clothing and bedding, with their personal belongings safeguarded by the maristān's treasurer (Al-Khitat al-Maqriziyyah, 1441, as cited in Hamarneh, 1962; as cited in Corbet, 1891). Medications, food, and physician visits were free to patients until they recovered fully. When patients were discharged, their personal possessions, including money and clothing, were returned to them (Al-Khitat al-Maqriziyyah, 1441, as cited in Ragab, 2015).

The bīmaristān primarily focused on acute care, distinguishing itself from long-term treatment facilities (Ragab, 2015). It was the first institution in Egypt to offer psychological treatment, featuring specialised wards for the mentally ill, complete with music therapy, and providing clothing and bedding similar to what was offered to the other patients (Koenig, 2005; Savage-Smith, 1994). Sultan Aḥmad ibn Ṭūlūn was also directly and consistently involved with the bīmaristān, often visiting patients after Friday prayers, including those with psychiatric conditions (Dols, 2006; Ragab, 2015). He routinely inspected the patients, inquired about their well-being, offered additional assistance, and sought God's forgiveness for them (Ragab, 2018). Remarkably, al-Fusṭāṭ Bīmaristān served Cairo for nearly six centuries (Hamarneh, 1962) (Figure 2.1).

Bīmaristān Nūr al-Dīn/Nūr al-Dīn (Est. 1154 CE)

The Turkish *Atabeg* (i.e., provincial governor) Nūr al-Dīn Maḥmūd Zangi (d.1174 CE) ruled Syria from 1154 to 1174 CE and played a crucial role in Muslim campaigns against the Crusaders (Zetterstéen, 2012). Renowned for his piety, Nūr al-Dīn was described by historian ibn Jubayr (d. 1217 CE) as one of the 'ascetic kings' who generously supported people, including strangers, knowledge seekers, people with low incomes, and pilgrims (Ibn Jubayr, 1185/1952). He established the Nūr al-Dīn Bīmaristān in Damascus in 1154 CE, placing it under the direction of physician Abū l-Majd ibn Abī l-Ḥakam (d. 1174 CE) and providing medications and food (Savage-Smith et al., 2020). This bīmaristān, located at the heart of the city, symbolically and physically placed the welfare of the people at the centre of urban life.

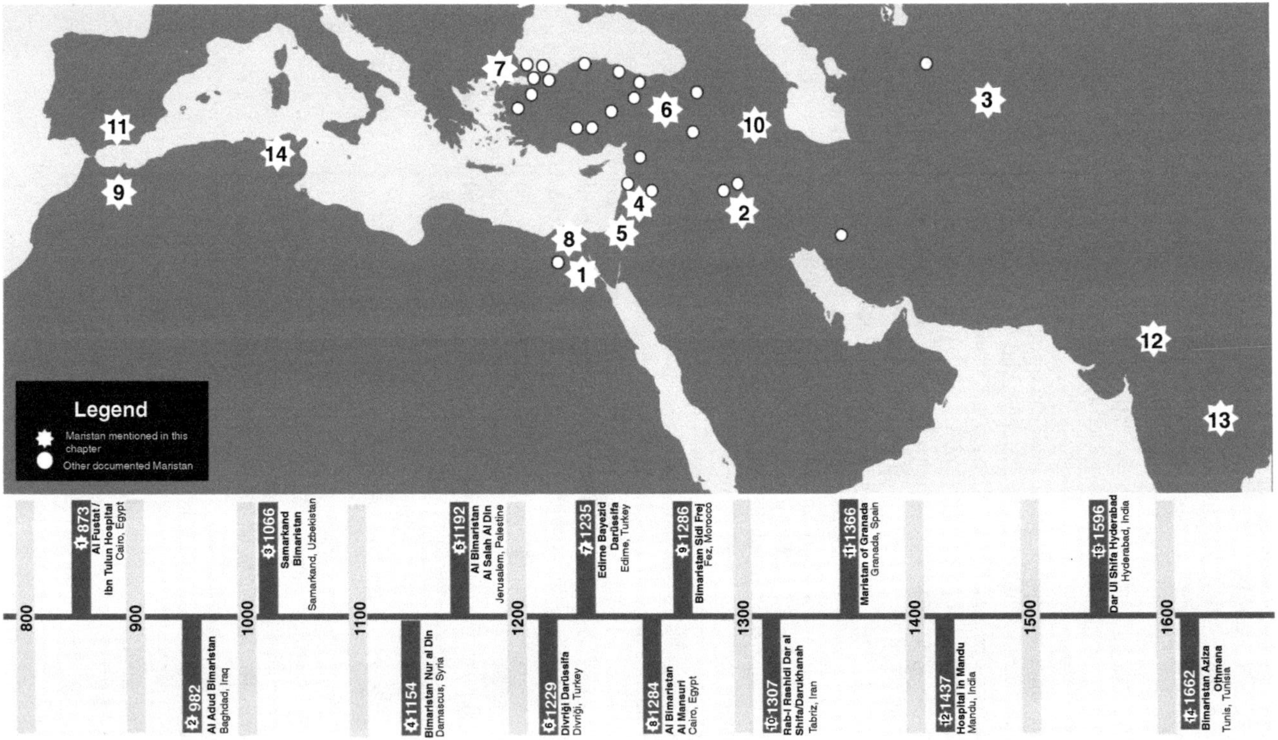

Figure 2.1. Visual representation of a selected group of maristāns with a timeline featuring the selected maristāns with dates of establishment and ruling period.

The Nūr al-Dīn Bīmaristān operated alongside a medical college, with Abū l-Majd appointed as its inaugural head (Hamarneh, 1962). Abū l-Majd regularly visited the hospital, devising treatment plans for superintendents and ward overseers to implement and then returning to the college to instruct students (Savage-Smith et al., 2020). Nūr al-Dīn enriched the bīmaristān by endowing it with an extensive medical library, enhancing its role in medical education, and facilitating medical discussions (Savage-Smith et al., 2020). This intense focus on medical education produced renowned physicians, including ibn Abī Uṣaybiʿah (d. 1270 CE), a prominent physician and medical historian, and ibn Nafs (d. 1288 CE), who was the first to describe pulmonary circulation (Hamarneh, 1962).

Bīmaristān Nūr al-Dīn, lauded by the renowned traveller ibn Jubayr, offered a generous daily allowance of fifteen dinars per day and maintained a patient registry, considered one of the earliest of its kind, documenting patients' names and their required medications, food, and other necessities (Ibn Jubayr, 1185/1952). References from ibn Jubayr and ibn Abī Uṣaybiʿah's works indicate provisions for treating the mentally ill and a dedicated ward for those suffering from mental illnesses. While detailed records of prescriptions and treatments have not survived, references to treatments such as opium and sound therapy for insomnia offer insights into the approaches taken for mental illnesses (Basuguy, 2019; Ibn Jubayr, 1185/1952; Ragab, 2015).

Ṣalāḥ al-Dīn Bīmaristān (Est. 1192 CE)

Ṣalāḥ al-Dīn Yūsuf ibn Ayyūb (d. 1193 CE), known as Saladin, ruled from 1137 to 1193 CE and was the founder of the Ayyubid Dynasty and Sultan of Egypt, Syria, Yemen, and Palestine. He was the face of the Islāmic opposition to the Crusades in the 12th century, notably reclaiming Jerusalem in 1187 CE (Sobernheim, 2012). Following the capture of Jerusalem, Ṣalāḥ al-Dīn endeavoured to reshape the city's identity from its Crusader past towards a revitalised Sunni Muslim character, all while preserving Christian holy sites and ensuring the well-being of Christian pilgrims (Abu-Munshar, 2007). In this transformation, he focused on reclaiming and restoring Islāmic buildings and holy sites, converting some former Christian establishments into new Islāmic ones. Among these projects was the founding of Ṣalāḥ al-Dīn Bīmaristān, constructed from part of a Crusader hospital complex in 1192 CE (Lemire, 2022). The bīmaristān, built within a converted church, included specialised rooms for different ailments and also served as a medical teaching institute (Sroor, 2010).

Insights from the Jerusalem *sijill*, the comprehensive collection of Ottoman-era court records spanning 1529–1917 CE, shed light on the 17th-century state of the bīmaristān. A waqf supervisor's request for funds to repair the bīmaristān provides crucial operational details, describing facilities such as a sick bay, mental institution, eye clinic, bath, and sitting rooms (Doumani, 1985; Ze'evi, 1996). A similar functional model likely applied to this Jerusalem-based bīmaristān, as found in the accounts of other bīmaristāns established by Ṣalāḥ al-Dīn. Ibn Jubayr's description of one in Cairo, for example, outlined a large ward for the insane, with attendants attending to patients' daily needs, offering insights into the probable operations of the Jerusalem Bīmaristān (Ibn Jubayr, 1185/1952; Basuguy, 2019).

Bīmaristān Qalāwūn/Al-Manṣūrī (Est. 1284 CE)

Qalāwūn aṣ-Ṣāliḥī (r. 1279–1290 CE), a former *mamlūk* (i.e., slave soldier) turned Sultan, established a lasting legacy through his patronage of the medical sciences, notably with the establishment of Bīmaristān al-Manṣūrī. This institution, originally a Fāṭimid palace, was considered Egypt's finest hospital and one of the most elaborate in the Islāmic world at the time (Dunlop et al., 2012). Being built in under a year, it could accommodate 8,000 individuals and featured specialised halls and wards for different genders and ailments, including fevers, eye diseases, surgical needs, and dysentery (Williams, 2008; Al-Khitat al-Maqriziyyah, 1441, as cited in Dunlop et al., 2012). An extensive waqf ensured the hospital an annual income of one million dirhams, supporting its operations (Kump, 1974).

The hospital boasted substantial administrative staff, lecture facilities, a chapel for Christian patients, and a rich library (Al-Khitat al-Maqriziyyah, 1441, as cited in Hamarneh, 1962). Bīmaristān al-Manṣūrī was inclusive, welcoming patients of all backgrounds, regardless of their wealth, status, age, sex, or condition. It was also equipped with a morgue, a pharmaceutical dispensary, and storerooms for preparing and storing drugs and ointments. Medical staff were assisted by employees responsible for maintaining cleanliness, attending to the sick, cooking, and facilitating comprehensive care (Ragab, 2015). The hospital's waqf deed detailed spending priorities, including its multifaceted operations, maintenance, medication, and medical tools. This extensive administration also spurred the development of a sophisticated medical record system, enhancing its managerial capabilities (Miller, 2006).

Notably, the bīmaristān prioritised comprehensive psychological well-being. Ibn Abī al-Bayān's (d. 1184 CE) *Pharmacopoeia of the hospital* (*Al-Dustūr al-Bīmaristānī*) detailed treatments for various mental illnesses, while the two psychiatric wards—one for women and the other for men—offered spiritual care, including Qur'ān readings and Islāmic teachings, with tailored sound therapy and water therapy in mental health wards (Porter, 1999; Williams, 2008; Hamarneh, 1962). Bīmaristān al-Manṣūrī's inclusive approach allowed patients, including those with chronic or mental health conditions, to stay as long as necessary for their recovery. Convalescent wards were available for those who needed to regain strength post-treatment (Miller, 2006). Additionally, departing patients, especially those in financial need, received grants to aid their reintegration into society, addressing mental and financial challenges (Ragab, 2015; Miller, 2006).

Persia and Mesopotamia

Al-ʿAḍudī Bīmaristān (Est. 982 CE)

ʿAḍud al-Dawlah (d. 983 CE) led the Buwayhid dynasty and governed regions including Iraq and parts of Central and Southern Iran from 949 to 983 CE (Bürgel Ch. & R., 1988). Recognised not only for consolidating his empire as the senior *amīr* (i.e., Muslim ruler) but also for his cultural contributions, his most notable achievement was the construction of the al-ʿAḍudī hospital in Baghdad, completed in 980 CE, just two years before his death (Hamarneh, 1962; Busse, 1975). Located strategically on the Tigris River's bend, the hospital served the most populous area of Baghdad and was renowned for its advanced medical equipment, comprehensive drug supplies, and extensive facilities (Savage-Smith et al., n.d.; Hamarneh, 1962).

This well-equipped institution was staffed by a medical team of eighty, including twenty-four specialised physicians. These experts covered a range of fields, such as ophthalmology, surgery, orthopaedics, and psychology, mainly focusing on treating mental illnesses (Elgood, 2010; Savage-Smith et al., n.d.). Despite common misconceptions, Abu Bakr al-Rāzī (d. 925 CE), a prominent physician known for his contributions to psychiatry, was not directly associated with al-ʿAḍudī but with an earlier hospital in Baghdad. Nonetheless, his influence on the medical practices at al-ʿAḍudī, particularly in psychiatric care, is evident and significant (Yilanli, 2018; Elgood, 2010).

Physicians at al-ʿAḍudī were distinguished for their approach to treatment, prescribing specific diets and actively involving students and interns in medical education, a practice reflective of al-Rāzī's methods (Savage-Smith et al., n.d.). The hospital's psychiatric ward, detailed in historical accounts by ibn Abī Uṣaybiʿah, implemented comprehensive treatment plans. These treatments included a holistic approach to mental health, utilising therapies such as diet, medication, occupational therapy, aromatherapy, baths, and sound therapy, all indicative of al-Rāzī's progressive influence on psychiatric care (Elgood, 2010; Yılanlı, 2018; Awaad et al., 2022).

Rab'-I Rashīdī Dār al-Shifāʾ/Dārukhanah (Est. 1307 CE)

Rashīd al-Dīn Faḍl Allāh (d. 1318 CE) was a physician, historian, and vizier to Maḥmūd Ghāzān (d. 1304 CE) of the Mongol dynasty in Iran who ruled from 1295 to 1304 CE ('Encyclopaedia Britannica,' 1998). After amassing a considerable fortune as a chief minister in the Il-khanid government, he utilised his wealth for several charitable initiatives (Blair, 2016; Khafipour, 2012). His most significant contribution was the Rab'-I Rashīdī complex in Tabrīz, encompassing mosques, tombs, a library, classrooms, a Sufi lodge, kitchens, a poor house, a hospice, and a hospital. Rashīd al-Dīn meticulously documented this complex's financial details and operations in the Rab'-I Rashīdī's endowment document drafted in 1309, *Waqf-nāmah-yi* Rab'-i Rashidi (Blair, 2016).

The Rab'-I Rashīdī complex's hospital, known as a dār al-shifā' or *dārukhanah* (house of medicine), was designed to serve the sick, poor, and destitute travellers. It featured specially designed areas, including a tonic house, pharmacy, patient halls, staff quarters, kitchen, and a rose-water storeroom (Al-Din Fazl Allāh, 1307). The hospital's funding included an annual endowment of 3,450 dinars, allocated to the hospital with key stipulations: 1,400 of which were used for the purchasing of medicine, 600 for food and the aid of the afflicted, 100 for burials, 200 for footwear, 200 for cotton used to employ widows, and the remaining 950 dinars for the salaries of hospital staff (Khafipour, 2012). The staff comprised a head physician, medical interns, a teaching assistant, a surgeon/ophthalmologist, an apothecary, a superintendent/treasurer, patient caretakers, a janitor, a doorman, and a cook (Blair, 2016; Khafipour, 2012).

Pharmacology was a focal point at the hospital, with the apothecary working alongside the physician and superintendent to determine prescriptions and prepare personalised drug treatment formulations. These preparations often included blends of opiates and herbal oil extracts and followed pharmacological treatises such as Dioscorides's *De Materia Medica* (On Medical Material; Khafipour, 2012). The hospital treated common ailments, including poisonings, kidney stones, liver pain, and inflammations. Additionally, the hospital strongly emphasised medical education, with physicians and assistants training medical interns over a five-year residency, equipping them to become licensed practitioners (Khafipour, 2012).

The chief physician, alongside his assistant, not only taught and actively tended to the sick, but also provided home consultations and necessary medications. The surgeon/ophthalmologist played a dual role in the hospital, conducting necessary surgeries and preparing ointments for any eye diseases presented. However, the hospital's waqf does not outline specific provisions for treating mental illnesses, focusing instead on a range of physical ailments and general healthcare needs (Khafipour, 2012).

Central Asia

Samarkand Bīmaristān (Est. 1066 CE)

Ibrāhīm ibn Naṣr Tamgach Khan (d. 1068 CE), who reigned from 1046 to 1068 CE, played a pivotal role in the stabilisation and economic growth of the Western Kara-Khanid Khanate, centred in Transoxiana's Samarkand (Bosworth, 1968). His reign was marked by a focus on internal order, security, respect for property, and promotion of trade and currency circulation, earning him a reputation as a devout and effective ruler (Khadr, 1967; Bosworth & Asimov, 1998). Capitalising on the economic prosperity achieved during his rule, Caliph Ibrāhīm ibn Naṣr initiated the development of a *madrasah* and a bīmaristān in Samarkand. Two *awqāf*, issued towards the end of his reign, detailed this initiative, with the bīmaristān receiving full approval around 1066 AD (Khadr, 1967).

The waqf outlined the bīmaristān's role as a sanctuary for the disadvantaged to alleviate their sickness and suffering. It was to serve the poor and weak, those afflicted by exile, misery, ordeal, or discouragement, without discrimination (Khadr, 1967). Notably, the waqf specified that the bīmaristān should cater to sick Muslims indefinitely until their illnesses or impoverished conditions improved. It also stated that those who recovered or were no longer indigent should vacate the facility to allow for the continuous care of others with temporary afflictions.

Details regarding the specific treatments offered in the bīmaristān are limited. However, the waqf deed elaborated on the maintenance, provisioning for patients, and treatments administered by medical professionals, including doctors and bloodletters. The waqf also covered the employment and treatment of personnel, including servants and cooks. As the donor, Caliph Ibrāhīm ibn Naṣr ensured that all patient needs, including food, drink, and medical supplies, were fully provided (Khadr, 1967). The bīmaristān's services included medicinal treatments, care from trained physicians, bloodletting, daily nourishment, and other patient-specific services. The dual functionality of the bīmaristān, offering both palliative and curative care, suggests that psychological care might also have been provided, particularly for chronic mental conditions.

North Africa and the Iberian Peninsula

Bīmaristān Sīdī Frej (Est. 1286 CE)

One of Abū Yūsuf Ya`qūb an-Nāṣr's (d. 1307 CE) most notable achievements as the ruler of Morocco's Marīnid dynasty (from 1286 to 1307 CE) was the establishment of the bīmaristān Sīdī Frej in Fez, the first and reportedly the largest bīmaristān in Morocco (Museum with No Frontiers [MWNF], 2001). Financed and maintained by his waqf, the bīmaristān Sīdī Fredj played a crucial role in shaping hospital development in Morocco and Spain, serving as a pioneering model for the integration of medical care and mental health treatment. The direct influence of Sīdī Fredj on the design and operation of the hospital for the mentally ill in Valencia, Spain, further demonstrates its lasting impact on the advancement of holistic healthcare in the Mediterranean and North African regions (Moussaoui & Glick, 2015).

The bīmaristān was distinguished by specialised sections for different ailments, including a significant portion dedicated to mental illnesses. It hosted eminent physicians such as ibn Rushd (d. 1198 CE) and was under the administrative oversight of Leon the African (d. 1554 CE; MWNF, 2001). Its proximity to herb shops facilitated the preparation of various medications. The bīmaristān adopted a Hippocratic approach to medicine, common in pre-modern Islāmic maristāns, which allowed for rationalistic patient treatment, particularly in psychiatry. It also incorporated empirical and scriptural methods, setting it apart from contemporary hospitals (Moussaoui & Glick, 2015).

Despite deterioration by the 19th century, the Sīdī Frej Bīmaristān's psychiatric treatment was comprehensive. Treatment options for mental illness were diverse and embodied the principle of healing rather than incarceration. Treatments included water, scent, and music therapy, with Andalusian music sessions conducted weekly to soothe psychiatric patients (Keller, 2005; Moussaoui & Glick, 2015). Beyond medical care, the bīmaristān likely served as a hub for a variety of public services, as it included an office for the lost and found and the court of the *muḥtasib*—the officer who supervises the observance of laws, punishes offenders, determines, investigates, and rectifies any injustices done to the public (Tourneau, 1949).

Maristān of Granada (Est. 1366 CE)

Prince Muḥammad ibn Yūsuf ibn Naṣr (d. 1391 CE), known as Muḥammad V, ascended to the throne as the eighth Nasrid ruler of the Emirate of Granada amidst a period of political unrest in 1354 CE. Though initially marked by turmoil, his reign saw a significant shift towards public welfare from 1365 to 1367 CE. Muḥammad V headed several public works projects, and under his rule, Granada flourished—growing to accommodate over 50,000 residents (Fábregas, 2020). Notable among his achievements was the establishment of the most fabulous hospital among Muslims in Spain, located in Granada (Hamarneh, 1962). Decreed as 'the seat of quick recovery' for the weak and the sick within the expansive city, Muḥammad V's maristān was a marker of the urban development and healthcare infrastructure characteristic of Nasrid rulership (Hamarneh, 1962; Imamuddīn, 1978).

The architecture of this maristān drew heavily from the bīmaristān Nūr al-Dīn in Damascus, featuring a layout that centred around a courtyard with a fountain or pool, a common design element in maristāns (Galton, 1997; Yahya, 1999). This maristān was a place for physical healing and included designated units for treating mental illnesses, indicative of the comprehensive medical approach adopted during this period (Pérez et al., 2013). The presence of water elements, namely pools and lion-shaped fountains, suggests hydrotherapy might have been an integral part of the treatment, especially for psychological ailments. Although specific details about the maristān's operations, including its original waqf document, remain elusive, it is reasonable to infer that it shared operational characteristics with contemporaneous maristāns across the Muslim World, such as the bīmaristān of Sīdī Frej (Pérez et al., 2012). These likely included the Hippocratic approach to medicine, provision of food, lodging, and medications to all seeking aid. The maristān of Granada stands today as the sole known remnant of the numerous Islāmic medical institutions that once dotted the Iberian Peninsula, which is a testament to the rich legacy of Islāmic medical and architectural heritage in Spain (Pérez et al., 2012).

Bīmaristān Aziza Othmana (Est. 1662 CE)

Fatima Othmana (d. 1669 CE), a princess of the Tunisian Muradid Dynasty (r. 1613–1705 CE), became affectionately known as 'Aziza' (beloved) Othmana after her extensive studies in *Sharī'ah* (i.e., Islāmic religious law), geopolitics, and the Qur'ān (Bessis, 2017). Following her Hajj pilgrimage, she used her wealth to endow 90,000 hectares of agricultural land through a waqf. This endowment was uniquely directed towards liberating enslaved people, ransoming prisoners, funding wedding trousseaux (bridal dowries or outfits) for poor young women, and most notably, establishing and funding her bīmaristān (Bessis, 2017).

Bīmaristān al-Azzafine, founded by Aziza Othmana in 1662 CE, was situated in the Musician's Souk, a lively bazaar in the Medina of Tunis. According to the waqf document, the bīmaristān welcomed everyone, irrespective of their creed or ethnicity, who was afflicted with sickness, wounds from sea travel, war, or invasions, or those who were destitute or without shelter. The hospital provided shelter and care until patients fully recovered (Essaddam, 2021). It featured a pharmacy, overseen by the head physician, offering treatments including serums, pastes, and ointments. Significant resources were allocated for maintaining cleanliness, including attendants who washed the sick and provided clean clothing. Additionally, the bīmaristān employed a chef with an attendant responsible for delivering food to each patient (Essaddam, 2021).

While the bīmaristān's documentation does not specify quarters or procedures for mentally ill patients, its inclusive policy and comprehensive caretaking capacity imply that those with mental afflictions were also cared for. Moreover, the choice of location in the Musician's Souk suggests a strategic use of the environmental element of music, potentially serving as a form of sound therapy to calm and soothe patients, thereby giving the bīmaristān an implicit provision of sound therapy.

Anatolia

Divriği Dār al-Shifā' (Est. 1229 CE)

Turan Melik, known as the 'Just Queen' of the Mengujekid dynasty (r. 1072–1277 CE) and daughter of Fakhr al-Dīn Bahramshāh (d.1225 CE), the most celebrated Mengujekid ruler, played a pivotal role in the development of Divriği. Her contributions, in collaboration with Mengujekid Sultan Aḥmadshah (d. 1251 CE), were instrumental in shaping the Divriği Dār al-Shifā'. This hospital-mosque complex, renowned for its exquisite architecture and charitable operations, stands as a testament to Islāmic architectural brilliance and a symbol of medical excellence in the Seljuk era (Pancaroğlu, 2009). The intricate designs and the emphasis on charity in constructing the dār al-shifā' highlight Turan Melik's commitment to aesthetic magnificence and societal welfare.

The Divriği Dār al-Shifā', founded around 1228–1229 CE, was built several decades after the Divriği Mosque, which itself was built following the Seljuk Turks' victory over the Byzantines in 1071 CE. The hospital was established as a healing sanctuary for the people of Divriği (Pancaroğlu, 2009). While the original waqf document detailing the hospital's operations and treatments remains undiscovered, the hospital's location on higher ground suggests a deliberate choice for cleaner airflow and an early understanding of environmental health factors. The dār al-shifā's architecture, adorned with vegetal, floral, and geometric stone reliefs, creates a visually tranquil environment, contributing to the therapeutic ambience (Centre, n.d.; Erdal & Erbaş, 2013; Pancaroğlu, 2009). These artistic elements served aesthetic purposes and likely played a role in promoting a calming atmosphere that is conducive to healing.

Remarkable in its approach to treatment, the Divriği Dār al-Shifā' was particularly noted for its use of sound therapy, especially for patients suffering from mental illnesses (Mihaljinec & Eser, 2022). This therapeutic method was supported by the architectural design of the dār al-shifā', which was structured to enhance the acoustics of music, thus maximising the therapeutic effects. The strategic design allowed for the harmonious diffusion of music throughout the establishment, creating a soothing and restorative auditory experience (Erdal & Erbaş, 2013). The integration of sound therapy into the hospital's treatment regimen illustrates an advanced understanding of the psychological aspects of healing, positioning the Divriği Dār al-Shifā' as a pioneer in holistic healthcare practices during its time.

Edirne Bayezid Dār al-Shifā' (Est. 1484 CE)

Bayezid II (d. 1512 CE)—the 8th Sultan of the Ottoman Empire and son of Meḥmed the Conqueror (d. 1481 CE)—ruled from 1481 to 1512 CE and was celebrated for his piety and philanthropy (Müderrisoğlu, 1991). After the conquest of Istanbul in 1453 CE, Edirne—the original capital of the Ottoman Empire—remained an important city for the Sultan and his royal military to stay when travelling to Europe during war times (Müderrisoğlu, 1991). During one of Sultan's visits to the city of Edirne, he had heard complaints from residents who requested the establishment of a hospital to serve the city's people. In response, Bayezid II established the third hospital of the Ottoman Empire and the first for the city of Edirne (Aktaş, 2010; Müderrisoğlu, 1991).

Constructed between 1484 and 1488 CE near the Tunca River, the dār al-shifā' was part of a grand complex, which consisted of a mosque, medical school, soup kitchen, bathhouse, library, water mill, bazaar, guesthouse, residential buildings, and a bridge that connected the overall complex to the rest of the city (Aktaş, 2010; Müderrisoğlu, 1991). Within the hospital were three interconnected courtyards, with the third being a hexagonal courtyard known as the inpatient clinic (paired with an inpatient psychiatric ward), featuring a central fountain and stage for musicians to deliver sound therapy to patients. It is also noted that the hospital's architecture inspired later medical architecture in Europe (Terzioğlu, 1999, as cited in Aktaş, 2010). In addition, the hospital was connected to a *madrasah*, which, in mediaeval usage, was essentially an institution of higher learning for many secular and non-secular subjects instead of one focused solely on the Islāmic sciences. In the context of the Edirne Dār al-Shifā', its *madrasah* functioned as a medical school providing theoretical education to students, who would then gain practical training and experience within the hospital (Müderrisoğlu, 1991).

The hospital staff consisted of three physicians, with one being the head physician, four nurses, one pharmacist, two cooks, one doorkeeper, one fragrance-maker, one maid, and one attendant who would wash and prepare the bodies of the deceased (Heybeli, 2009). An abundance of treatment options was available to psychiatric patients in the dār al-shifā'. Music therapy was a well-documented practice that would be provided to all patients housed within the hospital and was a particular source of remedy for those suffering from mental illnesses (Ergin, 2015; Heybeli, 2009). Aromatherapy was also employed, in which fragrances of various flowers during spring would be introduced to patients to soothe them alongside listening to bird songs (Evliya Celebi, 2006; Ersoy-Çak, & Özcan, 2018; Ergin, 2015). Water therapy would provide both a visual and sonic source of relaxation, promoting a sense of calmness for the patients (Evliya Celebi, 2006). In accounts by the famous Ottoman traveller Evliya Celebi (d. 1682 CE), who visited the hospital in 1653 CE, it was reported that while the dār al-shifā' initially served various medical needs, it primarily focused on psychological disorders, which was a transition that became more pronounced by 1866 CE (Müderrisoğlu, 1991).

South Asia

Hospital in Mandu (Est. 1437 CE)

Maḥmud Khiljī (d. 1469) ascended the throne in 1435 and ruled until 1469 CE, replacing the third king of the Ghori Dynasty, Muḥammad Ghori (d.1205 CE; Barnes, 1902). This marked the beginning of the Khiljī Dynasty, under which the kingdom of Malwa, encompassing the present-day Madhya Pradesh and southeastern Rajasthan, India, reached its zenith (Lane-Poole, 1903). Following his victorious campaigns, Sultan Maḥmud Khiljī returned to Mandu, his coronation city, to establish a large hospital. Financed through his personal funds and operating on royal land, the hospital was overseen by his physician, Maulāna Faḍl Allāh (d. n.d.). This institution functioned as a self-sustaining, charitable entity, though its architectural remains no longer exist. Nonetheless, historical records by the Persian historian Ferishta (d. 1620 CE) provide insights into the hospital's basic operations and facilities (Ferishta, 2013).

The Mandu Hospital catered to all patient classes, with dedicated wards and attendants. Notably, it provided separate apartments for those suffering from mental illnesses, marking an early recognition of the need for specialised psychiatric care. Detailed accounts of the psychiatric treatments offered are scarce, but it is known that patients with mania were housed separately within the hospital grounds to receive appropriate care (Ferishta, 2013). Due to this pioneering approach, it is regarded today as the first hospital with psychiatric care in the Indian subcontinent and far precedes the later establishment of insane asylums by the British East India Company in the 1600s (Sharma & Verma, 1985). Unlike the later asylums established by the British East Indian Company, which imported the Western model of primarily providing quarters for the insane, the Mandu Hospital provided both treatment and lodging, demonstrating a more holistic approach to mental healthcare (Mishra et al., 2018; Ferishta, 2013).

Dār al-shifā' Hyderabād (Est. 1596 CE)

Muḥammad Qulī Quṭb Shah (d. 1612 CE) was not only the fifth ruler of the Quṭb Shahī dynasty of Golconda (r. 1580–1612 CE) and the founder of Hyderabād, but also a poet and passionate advocate for cultural and medical advancements. Throughout his thirty-two-year reign, Muḥammad Qulī was known as a champion of cultural investment (Khan, 1996) and arguably the most important patron of medical studies in India at his time. He sponsored the composition of four medical treatises in Persian, reflecting his commitment to medical scholarship (Fabrizio Speziale, 2012). His most enduring contribution, however, was the establishment of the dār al-shifā' in Hyderabād, which ultimately cemented his legacy in medical patronage.

The dār al-shifā' of Hyderabād was built around 1595–1596 CE and was part of a *kulliyyah* (i.e., a complex of buildings centred around a mosque) that included a *ḥammām*, *caravanserai* (guesthouse for travellers), mosque, pharmacy, and *madrasah*. The complex was built near the garden Bāgh-i-Muḥammad Sahī and was said to accommodate up to 4,000 people. However, it is argued that this figure came about from a transcription error and that the entire complex likely served up to 400 people instead (Fabrizio Speziale, 2012). The hospital, still existing today as one of India's oldest remaining Islāmic hospitals, has about eighty rooms across four wings, spanning two floors, and is arranged around a courtyard (Fabrizio Speziale, 2012). Historical manuscripts described the hospital's physicians as endowed with 'the breath that brings life to the dying' (Mirza Hadi, 1858, f. 189v). Uniquely, the hospital offered competitive salaries to physicians, incentivising them to prioritise their duties at the dār al-shifā' over private practices (Mirza Hadi, 1858; Fabrizio Speziale, 2012).

Notably, the dār al-shifā' and *madrasah* were also described to have been used together as a medical education centre, with students present in both parts of the complex as part of their medical education (Mirza Hadi, 1858). While specific details about the treatments and medical curriculum remain scarce, the complex's design, featuring gardens and natural decorative motifs, suggests an emphasis on creating a soothing environment. This tranquil setting likely played a role in treating all patients, potentially including those with mental health conditions.

Conclusion

This exploration of the Islāmic world's maristāns reveals far more than a series of historical footnotes in healthcare. These institutions, scattered across a vast geographical landscape and spanning centuries, were not mere anomalies of generosity or progressive thought. Instead, they stand as towering testaments to a profound and shared ethos within the Islāmic civilisation—a conviction that providing unconditional care to the destitute and afflicted is not just an act of charity but a fundamental expression of piety and profound human empathy. This ethos was embraced by governments, rulers, and philanthropists alike, who saw in these maristāns an opportunity to leave a lasting mark of compassion and societal advancement.

The striking commonalities among these maristāns—in their treatment methodologies, architectural elegance, or operational blueprints—reveal a deeply ingrained philosophy of care that transcended regional and chronological borders. These maristāns were much more than healthcare centres; they were beacons of hope and healing hubs that uplifted entire communities, enhancing the quality of life for residents and weary travellers alike. They secured not only the legacy of their patrons but also etched an enduring narrative of benevolence and welfare in the annals of Islāmic history.

Furthermore, these maristāns were at the forefront of a progressive perspective on mental health, a view far ahead of its time. They championed a holistic approach to mental well-being, weaving this advanced understanding into the very fabric of their care. This dedication to comprehensive mental healthcare, consistent across countless maristāns, cements these institutions as monumental pillars of Islāmicate (associated with Muslims rather than directly with the religion of Islām) medicine and Islāmic intellectual heritage. Thus, these maristāns emerge not just as historical landmarks but as enduring symbols of an enlightened civilisation that valued and nurtured its people's physical and mental well-being, setting a benchmark in healthcare that resonates through the ages.

Note

1 In the context of the Islāmic world, the term 'slave' (*Qur'ānically*: *mā malakat aymānukum*—literally 'those whom your right hands possess') referred to individuals who were legally owned by another person and compelled to work or serve their owner. Slavery in Islāmic societies, however, was distinct from the way it is commonly understood today. While it is essential to note that practices varied across time and regions, slavery in Islāmic societies generally had certain characteristics that distinguished it from other forms of slavery. Slavery in Islāmic societies was regulated by *Sharī'ah* law, which provided guidelines for the treatment of slaves and their rights such as the right to marry, have children, and own property. Slaves in Islāmic societies were often acquired through conquest, debt, or as a result of being born to slave parents. They could be used for various purposes, including domestic service, agricultural labour, military service, and administrative roles. Slavery in Islāmic societies was also distinct from modern comprehension, with slaves having opportunities for social mobility, education, and even positions of influence and power. Islāmic law strictly encouraged the humane treatment of slaves, and it was considered a virtuous act for a Muslim to free a slave, either through manumission or as an act of charity (Brunschvig, 2012).

References

Abu-Munshar, M. Y. (2007). *Islamic Jerusalem and Its Christians: A History of Tolerance and Tensions*. Bloomsbury Academic.

Aktaş, S. (2010). XV. Ve XVI. Yüzyıllarda Sultan Dârüşşifâları. Master's Thesis, Gazi University.

Al-Din Fazl Allāh, R. (1307). *Waqf-namah-yi Rab'-i Rashidi*. https://en.unesco.org/silkroad/silk-road-themes/documentary-heritage/deed-endowment-rab-i-rashidi-rab-i-rashidi-endowment-13th

Awaad, R., Conn, Y. S., Kolkailah, N., El-Haddad, H., Ali, S., & Fereydooni, S. (2022). From alchemy to psychiatry: A glimpse into the ethics and mental health practices of tenth-century Muslim physician Abū Bakr al-Rāzī. *Harvard review of psychiatry*, *30*(5), 323–326. https://doi.org/10.1097/HRP.0000000000000347

Barnes, E. (1902). *Dhar & Mandu: A Guide*. Society's Library.

Basuguy, B. (2019). Medical developments during the reign of salah al-dîn al-ayyûbî and the famous physicians of the period. *Journal of Research on History of Medicine*, *8*(1), 3–18.

Bessis, S. (2017). *Les Valeureuses: Cinq Tunisiennes dans l'Histoire*. Elyzad.

Blair, S. S. (2016). RAB'-E RAŠIDI. In *Encyclopædia Iranica*. https://www.iranicaonline.org/articles/rab-e-rashidi

Bosworth, C. E. (1968). À propos de deux actes de waqf. Journal *Asiatique*, *256*, 449–455.

Bosworth, C. E., & Asimov, M. S. (Eds.). (1998). *History of civilizations of central Asia: Vol. IV*. United Nations Educational, Scientific and Cultural Organization.

Brunschvig, R. (2012). 'Abd. In *Encyclopaedia of Islam* (2nd ed.). Brill. https://referenceworks.brillonline.com/entries/encyclopaedia-of-islam-2/abd-COM_0003

Bürgel Ch., & R., M. (1988). 'ażod-Al-Dawla, Abū Šojā' Fannā Ḵosrow. In *Encyclopædia Iranica: Vol. III*. https://www.iranicaonline.org/articles/azod-al-dawla-abu-soja

Busse, H. (1975). Iran under the Būyids. In R. N. Frye (Ed.), *The Cambridge history of Iran: The Period from the Arab Invasion to the Saljuqs* (Vol. 4, pp. 250–304//262–287). Cambridge University Press. https://doi.org/10.1017/CHOL9780521200936.008

Corbet, E. K. (1891). The life and works of Aḥmad ibn Ṭūlūn. *Journal of the Royal Asiatic Society of Great Britain and Ireland*, 531. http://www.jstor.org/stable/25197067

Dols, M. W. (2006). The treatment of the Insane. *Journal of Muslim Mental Health*, *1*(2), 185–203. https://doi.org/10.1080/15564900600980830

Doumani, B. B. (1985). Palestinian Islamic court records: A source for socioeconomic history. *Middle East Studies Association Bulletin*, *19*(2), 155–172. https://doi.org/10.1017/S0026318400016114

Dunlop, D. M., Colin, G. S., & Şehsuvaroğlu, B. N. (2012). *Bīmāristān*. In *Encyclopaedia of Islam* (2nd ed.). Brill. https://referenceworks.brillonline.com/entries/encyclopaedia-of-islam-2/bimaristan-COM_0123?s.num=61&s.rows=100

Elgood, C. (Ed.). (2010). The rise of the Buwayhid family. In *A Medical History of Persia and the Eastern Caliphate: From the Earliest Times until the Year A.D. 1932* (pp. 144–183). Cambridge University Press. https://doi.org/10.1017/CBO9780511710766.007

Erdal, G., & Erbaş, İ. (2013). Darüşşifas where music therapy was practiced during Anatolian Seljuks and Ottomans/Selçuklu ve Osmanlı Darüşşifalarında Müzikle Tedavi. *Tarih Kültür ve Sanat Araştırmaları Dergisi*, *2*(1), 1–19. https://www.researchgate.net/publication/307817485_Darussifas_Where_Music_Threapy_was_Practiced_During_Anatolian_Seljuks_and_Ottomans_Selcuklu_ve_Osmanli_Darussifalarinda_Muzikle_Tedavi

Ergin, N. (2015). Healing by design? An experiential approach to early modern Ottoman hospital architecture. *Turkish Historical Review*, *6*(1), 1–37. https://doi.org/10.1163/18775462-00601001

Ersoy-Çak, Ş., & Özcan, N. (2018). Müzik terapinin tarihsel gelişimi ve uygulandığı mekânlara bir bakış [A look into the historical development of music therapy and places of its implementation]. *Turkish Studies-Social Sciences*, *13*(18), 599–618. https://doi.org/10.7827/TurkishStudies.14112

Essaddam, H. (2021, April 28). *La Fondation du Bimaristan Al-Azzafine*. Medical History.

Evliya Çelebi. (2006). Günümüz Türkçesiyle Evliya Çelebi Seyahatnamesi. In (Eds.), Y. Dagli & S. A. Kahraman (Trans.), *Travelbook of Evliya Çelebi in Modern Turkish* (Vol. 1). Yapı Kredi Yayınları.

Fábregas, A. (2020). *The Nasrid Kingdom of Granada between East and West: Thirteenth to Fifteenth Centuries*. Brill. https://books.google.com/books?id=zgsOEAAAQBAJ

Fabrizio Speziale. (2012). *Hospitals in Iran and India, 1500–1950s* (Issue v. 7). Brill. https://stanford.idm.oclc.org/login?url=https://search.ebscohost.com/login.aspx?direct=true&db=e025xna&AN=456496&site=ehost-live&scope=site

Ferishta, M. K. (2013). J. Briggs (Trans.), *History of the Rise of the Mahomedan Power in India, till the Year AD 1612* (Vol. 3). Cambridge University Press. https://doi.org/10.1017/CBO9781139506670

Galton, D. J. (1997). Destruction of a hospital. *Journal of the Royal Society of Medicine*, *90*(7), 406–408. https://doi.org/10.1177/014107689709000713

Hamarneh, S. (1962). Development of hospitals in Islam. *Journal of the History of Medicine and Allied Sciences*, *17*(3), 366–384. JSTOR.

Hassan, Z. M. (2012). Aḥmad b. Ṭūlūn. In *Encyclopaedia of Islam* (2nd ed.). Brill. https://referenceworks.brillonline.com/entries/encyclopaedia-of-islam-2/ahmad-b-tulun-SIM_0398

Heybeli, N. (2009). Sultan Bayezid II Külliyesi: One of the earliest medical schools: Founded in 1488. *Clinical Orthopaedics & Related Research*, *467*(9), 2457–2463. https://doi.org/10.1007/s11999-008-0645-1

Imamuddīn, S. M. (1978). Māristān (hospitals) in medieval Spain. *Islamic Studies*, *17*(1), 45–55. JSTOR.

Keller, R. C. (2005). Pinel in the Maghreb: Liberation, Confinement, and Psychiatric Reform in French North Africa. *Bulletin of the History of Medicine*, *79*(3), 459–499. https://doi.org/10.1353/bhm.2005.0112

Khadr, M. (1967). Deux Actes de Waqf D'un Qarahanide D'Asie Centrale. *Journal Asiatique*, *255*, 305–335.

Khafipour, H. (2012). A Hospital in Ilkhānid Iran: Toward a Socio-economic Reconstruction of the Rab'-i Rashīdī. *Iranian Studies*, *45*(1), 97–117. https://doi.org/10.1080/00210862.2011.573996

Khan, M. H. (1996). *Mohammad Quli Qutb Shah*. Sahitya Akademi.

Koenig, H. G. (2005). *Faith and Mental Health*. Templeton Press. https://www.loc.gov/item/2016397784/

Kump, W. L. (1974). Historic hospitals. Financing the Maristan of Qalaun. *Minnesota Medicine*, *57*(6), 464.

Lane-Poole, S. (1903). *Mediaeval India under Mohammedan Rule (A.D. 712–1764)*. T. Fisher Unwin. https://books.google.com/books?id=Iqgjsyl969wC

Lemire, V. (2022). *Jerusalem: History of a Global City*. University of California Press. https://books.google.com/books?id=OlhYEAAAQBAJ

McClary, R. P. (2021). *Dar al-shifa'or Bimaristan? Medieval Islamic Hospitals of Damascus, Sivas and Cairo in the 12th and 13th Centuries*. In M. Gharipour (Ed.), *A Matter for Life and Death* (pp. 99–115). Bloomsbury Publishing.

Mihaljinec, I., & Eser, E. (2022). Divriği hospital: Medieval healing venue and its acoustic characteristics. *Randwick International of Social Science Journal*, *3*(1), *1*. https://doi.org/10.47175/rissj.v3i1.376

Miller, A. C. (2006). Jundi-Shapur, Bimaristans, and the rise of academic medical centres. *Journal of the Royal Society of Medicine*, *99*(12), 615–617. https://doi.org/10.1177/014107680609901208

Mirza Hadi. (1858). *Tarikh-i Qut b-i Shahiyah* (Folio 189v). https://www.loc.gov/item/2016397784/

Mishra, A., Mathai, T., & Ram, D. (2018). History of psychiatry: An Indian perspective. *Industrial Psychiatry Journal*, *27*(1), 21–26. https://doi.org/10.4103/ipj.ipj_69_16

Moussaoui, D., & Glick, I. D. (2015). The Maristan "Sidi Fredj" in Fez, Morocco. *American Journal of Psychiatry*, *172*(9), 838–839. https://doi.org/10.1176/appi.ajp.2015.15010051

Müderrisoğlu. (1991). *Edirne 2. Bayezid Kulliyesi*. https://acikerisim.fsm.edu.tr/xmlui/bitstream/handle/11352/375/M%C3%BCderriso%20lu.pdf?sequence=1

Muḥammadibn Aḥmad, called Ibn Jubair, 1145–1217. (1952). R. J. C. Broadhurst (Trans.), The Travels of Ibn Jubayr: A Mediaeval Journey from Cordoba to Jerusalem. Bloomsbury Publishing (Original work dated 1185).

Musée Sans Frontières. (2001). *Le Maroc Andalou: A la découverte d'un Art de Vivre* (2nd ed.). Musée Sans Frontières.

Pancaroğlu, O. (2009). The Mosque-hospital complex in Divriği: A history of relations and transitions. *Anadolu ve Cevresinde Ortaçağ*, *3*, 169–198.

Pérez, J., Baldessarini, R. J., Undurraga, J., & Sánchez-Moreno, J. (2012). Origins of psychiatric hospitalisation in medieval Spain. *Psychiatric Quarterly*, *83*(4), 419–430. https://doi.org/10.1007/s11126-012-9212-8

Pérez, J., Girón-Irueste, F., Gurpegui, M., Baldessarini, R. J., & de Leon, J. (2013). The lions of granada maristan. *American Journal of Psychiatry*, *170*(2), 152–153. https://doi.org/10.1176/appi.ajp.2012.12081066

Porter, R. (1999). *The Greatest Benefit to Mankind: A Medical History of Humanity*. W. W. Norton. https://books.google.com/books?id=zcpFAAAAQBAJ

Ragab, A. (2015). *The Medieval Islamic Hospital: Medicine, Religion, and Charity*. Cambridge University Press. https://doi.org/10.1017/CBO9781316271797

Ragab, A. (2018). Illness and the hospital in the Muslim city: Reflections on the pietistic space of illness in premodern Islam. *Journal of Islamic and Muslim Studies*, *3*(2), 1–20.

Saheeh International. (n.d.). *English Translation of the Meaning of the Holy Qur'ān*. Conveying Islāmic Message Society.

Savage-Smith, E. (1994). *Islamic Culture and the Medical Arts: Hospitals* [Exhibitions]. U.S. National Library of Medicine. https://www.nlm.nih.gov/exhibition/islamic_medical/islamic_12.html

Savage-Smith, E., & S. Swain, &van Gelder, G. J. (Eds.). (2020). *A Literary History of Medicine*. Brill. https://doi.org/10.1163/37704_0668IbnAbiUsaibia.Tabaqatalatibba.lhom-tr-eng1

Sharma, S., & Verma, L. P. (1985). History of mental hospitals in indian sub-continent. In P. Pichot, P. Berner, R. Wolf, & K. Thau (Eds.), *Psychiatry The State of the Art: History of Psychiatry, National Schools, Education, and Transcultural Psychiatry* (Vol. 8, pp. 45–52). Springer. https://doi.org/10.1007/978-1-4757-1853-9_6

Sobernheim. (2012). Saladin. In *Encyclopaedia of Islam First Edition (1913–1936)*. Brill. https://referenceworks.brillonline.com/entries/encyclopaedia-of-islam-1/saladin-SIM_5097

Sroor, M. (2010). *Métamorphose de biens waqfs en propriété privée à Jérusalem (1858–1917)*. In *Fondations pieuses en mouvement: De la transformation du statut de propriété des biens waqfs à Jérusalem (1858–1917)* (pp. 261–297). Presses de l'Ifpo. https://books.openedition.org/ifpo/1299

Tourneau, R. L. (1949). Fès avant le protectorat: Étude économique et sociale d'une ville de l'occident musulman. *SMLE*. https://books.google.com/books?id=KsIvAAAAIAAJ

UWH Centre (n.d.). Great Mosque and Hospital of Divriği. UNESCO World Heritage Centre. Retrieved December 26, 2022, from https://whc.unesco.org/en/list/358/

Williams, C. (2008). *Islamic Monuments in Cairo: The Practical Guide*. American University in Cairo Press. https://books.google.com/books?id=rREnDAAAQBAJ

Yahya, A. (1999). Common architectural characteristics in the planning and development of the Bimaristan in the Arab and Islamic eras. *Athar Alrafedain*, *3*(2), 187–224. https://doi.org/10.33899/athar.1999.164572

Yilanli, M. (2018). Muḥammad ibn Zakariya al-Razi and the first psychiatric ward. *American Journal of Psychiatry Residents' Journal*, *13*(9), 11–11. https://doi.org/10.1176/appi.ajp-rj.2018.130905

Ze'evi, D. (1996). *Ottoman Century, An: The District of Jerusalem in the 1600s*. SUNY Press. https://stanford.idm.oclc.org/login?url=https://search.ebscohost.com/login.aspx?direct=true&db=nlebk&AN=5300&site=ehost-live&scope=site

Zetterstéen, K. V. (2012). Nūr al-Dīn. In *Encyclopaedia of Islam, First Edition (1913–1936)*. Brill. https://referenceworks.brillonline.com/entries/encyclopaedia-of-islam-1/nur-al-din-SIM_3530

3 Finance, Administration, and Maintenance of Services in Maristāns

Merve Nursoy-Demir and Salma Albezreh

Financial System: Establishment and Sustainability through Waqf

The Fundamentals of Waqf

The endurance of the maristān establishment across centuries of Islāmicate rule stemmed from the Islāmically inspired financial system called waqf (Ansari, 2013; Dişli, 2015; Hamarneh, 1962; Lev, 2005). The Arabic word waqf means to hold or possess, while the term waqf explicitly denotes both the act of endowment and the endowed property itself (Günay, 2012). The waqf system was the primary financial mechanism for societal provisions within Islāmic civilisations. However, charitable Islāmic endowment should not be confused with modern social welfare. Waqfs were self-motivated private initiatives (Lev, 2005). As a legally systematised institution, the waqf is a unique invention of Islāmic civilisation (Akyıldız & Abay, 2017). Scholars have debated the historical origins of the waqf system and whether Byzantine charity institutions inspired pious Islāmic endowments (Dols, 1984; Peters et al., 2012). However, there is no significant evidence to suggest that pre-Islāmic charity models inspired the Islāmic waqf system, particularly for the endowment of hospitals (Ansari, 2013).

The fiqh (Islāmic jurisprudence) of waqf developed over centuries into a highly sophisticated legal system with detailed codes of operation (Günay, 2012; Peters et al., 2012). There are varying opinions regarding the application of the waqf system across different schools of thought in Islāmic fiqh (Günay, 2012). However, scholars generally agree upon four legally required components that must be specified in a waqf: (1) the declaration of intention, (2) the sponsoring agent, (3) the endowed property, and (4) the waqf's beneficiaries (Günay, 2012). According to Islāmic law, a waqf is formed when a mentally sound adult declares an intention to dedicate a specified portion of their property to a defined group of beneficiaries (i.e., person or public) as an act of piety (Peters et al., 2012). The financial source of the waqf must be halal

DOI: 10.4324/9781003329589-3

(i.e., Islāmically permissible) and free of debt or bankruptcy. Additionally, the endower must be a free individual in full possession of their wealth, and the described goal of the waqf must be religiously appropriate. Waqfs, in principle, were also irrevocable and incessant (Khan, 2015). Notably, there was no legal requirement for the sponsors or recipients of the waqf to be Muslim (Günay, 2012; Peters et al., 2012).

Two main types of waqf endured. The *ṣaḥīḥ* (authentic) waqf consisted of private property permanently endowed for the defined service. The second type of waqf, called *irṣādī* (earmark) waqf, denoted endowments that were established on state property for communal services, including but not limited to education, healthcare, or social justice advocacy (Akgündüz, 2000). The funds for *irṣādī* waqfs were drawn from the state treasury according to the authorisation of the presiding ruler. While the physical property remained under the state's ownership, its usage rights and the revenue it produced were reserved for the waqf's social welfare purposes (Akgündüz, 2000; Günay, 2012).

Maristāns were endowed with a range of resources, including but not limited to land (e.g., villages and agricultural lands) and material collections (e.g., medical books and musical instruments). These endowments were categorised into primary and secondary types, with the former consisting of the physical infrastructure of the hospital, including the land on which it stood, and the latter consisting of commercial estates, equipment, additional land for future expansion and renovation projects, and supplementary materials (Ansari, 2013). The primary sources of income for maristāns, in addition to its assigned waqfs, included rent received from residential dwellings, markets, shops, and bathhouses, as well as revenue generated from agricultural produce (McClary, 2021; Necipoğlu, 2013).

Waqfs not only characterised the design of Islāmicate cities but they also influenced the cultural fabric of Muslim societies (Bayartan, 2008; Demir, 2019). They established the backbone for institutionalised public service in Islāmicate civilisations. Waqfs significantly reduced the state's social welfare expenditures and deliberately served the community in areas where the expenses exceeded what the public could afford (Akman, 2020; Bayartan, 2008). Common examples of waqf-based institutions besides maristāns include mosques, *madrasahs*, caravanserais, and Sufi lodges (Bayartan, 2008; McClary, 2021). In addition to such grand constructions of social welfare, charitable endowments made numerous other services conceivable, such as the construction and distribution of drinking fountains, the provision of funeral services for the kinless, the operation of *ḥammāmāt* (communal bath houses) free of charge, and the allocation of reception services for pilgrim caravans (Bayartan, 2008). However, maristāns persistently established themselves as signature institutions among the various subsidiary charity organisations that the waqf system founded (Ahmed, 2007).

The Motivation behind the Establishment of Waqfs

Sharīʿah—the code of divine law that originates from the two Islāmic primary sources: Qurʾān and Ḥadīth—served as the primary force behind the creation of a community-facing system of endowments due to its recurring theme of philanthropy (Calder & Hooker, 2012; Surty, 1997). In its overarching and comprehensive nature, the impact of *Sharīʿah* on Muslims' actions was not only on an individual level but also on societal and political levels (Keshavarzi & Ali, 2019). The Qurʾān and Ḥadīth both emphasise serving vulnerable individuals: the poor, the ill, and the traveller (*The Qurʾān*, 9:60; 63;10). Even though the Qurʾān does not explicitly mention the term waqf, frequent references to charity as a permanent source of reward (*The Qurʾān*, 3:92) are interpreted as reference points for the formation of waqfs (Şentürk, 2010).

The Prophet Muḥammad (ﷺ) also identified *ṣadaqah jāriyah* (charity) as one of the three ways to extend continuous *thawāb* (reward) beyond one's lifetime (Saḥīḥ Muslim, 1631). The founders of waqfs believed that by endowing social welfare institutions, they would fulfil the rights of the needy, gain the prayers of others, and ultimately reap returns in the form of personal salvation (Lev, 2005). Thus, the earliest models of waqfs were found in the lifetime of the Prophet Muḥammad (ﷺ), as put into practice by the Messenger (ﷺ) himself. Members of the Prophet Muḥammad's (ﷺ) own family and *ṣaḥābah* (companions) were reported to have offered charity in a waqf-like fashion (Şentürk, 2010). For example, in a narrative reported by ibn ʿUmar, ʿUmar ibn al-Khaṭṭāb (d. 644 CE) was advised by the Prophet Muḥammad (ﷺ) to donate the yield of one of his properties while maintaining his ownership of the land (Saḥīḥ Muslim, 1632a).

In addition to religious motives, historical sources reveal a combination of political, social, economic, and personal motives behind the endowment of hospitals (Ansari, 2013). The practice became widespread among the upper class, who considered the funding of hospitals as a highly prestigious act in which the most powerful of the community (e.g., sultans, royal family members, or high-ranking officials) participated (McClary, 2021). Politically, rulers would enjoy the prestige of sponsoring monumental endowments like maristāns that immortalised their power years after their rule ceased. Socially, establishing welfare institutions for those in need decorated their reputation as just and compassionate patrons in the public eye (Akyıldız & Abay, 2017). Economically, endowed properties were often exempt from taxation or seizure by creditors and the state (Akyıldız & Abay, 2017).

Personal experiences also played a role in motivating people of wealth to sponsor maristāns. For instance, Hürrem Sultan (d. 1558 CE) sponsored Haseki Dār al-Shifā' after caring for a disabled child who suffered from adverse health conditions (Necipoğlu, 2013). In another example, Sultan al-Manṣūr (d. 1603 CE) built the Qalāwūn Bīmaristān in Cairo after being impressed by the exceptional medical care he received as a patient at the

Nūr al-Dīn Bīmaristān in Damascus (Hamarneh, 1962). Thus, maristāns were endowed for a variety of explicit and implicit reasons that popularised the act of endowment to all those who could afford it.

Financial Sustainability of Maristān Waqfs

The majority of Muslim scholars held the view that waqfs ought to be everlasting (Khan, 2015); therefore, rulers and affluent members of society were responsible for ensuring that endowments did not cease to provide a sufficient stream of income to cover their respective project's costs (Günay, 2012; Lev, 2005). This foresighted facet of the waqf system played a crucial role in ensuring the survival of maristāns beyond their founders' lifetimes and for centuries to come.

It is important to note that the free services patients received in maristāns exceeded medical treatment. Other complimentary amenities associated with hospital admission included prescribed medications, food, bedding, clothing items, *ḥammām* services, and accommodation services for patients' guests to stay in *imarets* (guesthouses) (Lev, 2005). For maristāns to offer such services without discrimination, they required dynamic and renewable sources of income, including the introduction of new sponsors. Prominent maristāns such as al-ʿAḍudī and Qalāwūn were able to attract new sponsors to focus on restoring hospital buildings and continuing services (Lev, 2005). Rulers and state authorities were among those who advocated for the contemporary undertaking of old waqfs (Bayartan, 2008). Although there were few sponsors, they commonly donated large amounts (Lev, 2005).

Another process that corroborated the financial sustainability of maristāns was the exchange of former waqf assets for newly appreciated income sources to adjust to the inevitable ebb and flow of the economic theatre. Qāḍī (local judges) were given the authority to replace any financially dysfunctional properties with more fruitful ones. This practice allowed maristāns to maintain financial equilibrium and avoid the depreciation of the original endowment (Lev, 2005).

Sponsors of Maristāns

Sponsors of maristāns were usually caliphs, rulers, and members of the royal family who constituted the highest segment of the societal hierarchy (Akman, 2020; Altıntaş, 2022; Hamarneh, 1962). Monumental maristāns such as Granada, Qalāwūn, Fatih, and Edirne Bayezid were all sponsored by the grand sultans of their times (Hamarneh, 1962; McClary, 2021). Additionally, high-ranking officials, governors, viziers, commanders, noblemen, and sometimes physicians contributed to the establishment, renovation, and extension of maristāns (Ansari, 2013). For instance, the notable Nūr al-Dīn

Maristān of Damascus was founded by Nūr al-Dīn al-Zangi (d. 1174 CE) when he was an *Aṭābey* (provincial governor; Kök, 2007). In addition to the grand maristāns built across Islāmicate capital cities, there were modestly sized maristāns built by royal family members or viziers in smaller urban towns—such as the Amasya and Manisa maristāns in Anatolia (Altıntaş, 2022; Lev, 2005).

Numerous women were also active participants in this endeavour, donating a significant portion of their wealth to waqfs (Demir, 2019). Female members of royal families played a key role in establishing multiple long-lasting waqfs (Akman, 2020; Ansari, 2013). Interestingly, hospitals were among the most common entities to which women devoted their endowments (Demir, 2019). Examples of female sponsorship in maristāns include but are not limited to the Ottoman hospitals Manisa Hafsa Sultan Dār al-Shifā' (est. 1539 CE) and Haseki Sultan Dār al-Shifā' (Ünver, 1939), the Anatolian Seljuk era hospital Divriği Sultan Melik Dār al-Shifā' (est. 1228 CE; Demir, 2019), the Ilkhanid-era hospital Amasya Dār al-Shifā' (est. 1308 CE), and the Mouradite-era (1613–1702 CE) hospital Bīmaristān Aziza Othmana in Tunisia. The signature feature of all these maristāns sponsored by women was the psychiatric care they provided for the public.

After being founded, maristāns occasionally received endowments from laypeople (Lev, 2005). One such instance was recorded for the al-ʿAḍudī Hospital in Baghdad. Approximately one hundred years after its establishment, a prominent resident of Baghdad named Abū Manṣūr ibn Yūsuf restored al-ʿAḍudī Hospital by initiating a new set of endowments, reconstructing the building, and assembling a team of physicians (Lev, 2005). These examples serve to demonstrate how supervision and sponsorship of hospital endowments could undergo transitions to ensure the continuation of services.

Beneficiaries of Maristāns

Historical sources report that most hospitalised patients came from financially disadvantaged backgrounds, thus lacking the social and financial resources to access medical care from private practitioners in their homes, which was the typical practice in pre-modern history (Altıntaş, 2022; Hamarneh, 1962; Taşkıran, 1972). In addition, non-residents who were travellers, traders, or commissioned officials commonly sought out medical services in maristāns (Altıntaş, 2022). Homecare presented unique challenges for the mentally ill and their caretakers, depending on the nature of their illness (e.g., harm to oneself, harm to others, psychotic episodes). In one example, Sarı (2016) translates a documented case of a Christian man petitioning the court for his son's entry into a maristān due to self-harming behaviour:

> A Christian named Hâsır applied to the court. He wanted his son, who had attempted suicide, to be hospitalised. Hilmi Beşe, the guardian of Sultan

> Alâeddin Hospital, was present at the hearing of the case. The father said, 'My son Mirat, who is present here, has symptoms of madness. He threw himself down a well and in other dangerous places. I wish him to be handed over to Hilmi Beşe for treatment.' Madness was displayed in Mirat's manners and behaviour. In addition, local residents confirmed Mirat's insanity and also reported about him throwing himself into the well, whereupon the father delivered his son to the official Hilmi Beşe to be treated at the hospital. (Sarı 2016, p. 60)

Hence, there were systems in place through which society members could request institutional care for the patient at the expense of the state (Sarı, 2008; Scalenghe, 2014; Taşkıran, 1972). As a result, maristāns became critical healing spaces for people with severe psychiatric disorders.

While most inpatient units were predominantly available for men, there were often separate wards, bathrooms, and courtyards for female patients (Ataseven, 1985; Dişli, 2021). For example, Qalāwūn Maristān in Cairo and Bīmaristān Arġūn Al-Kāmilī (est. 1354 CE) in Aleppo had two wards dedicated to psychiatric conditions, one for women and one for men (Issa, 1928). The gendering of space in maristāns was a matter of medical ethics, privacy, and Islāmic legality (Dişli, 2021). For instance, if the only doctor available was male, it was often deemed permissible for him to examine and treat female patients despite not qualifying as a maḥram (non-marriageable relative), per Islāmic law (Dişli, 2021). Nonetheless the inclusion of female patient populations often coincided with the onboarding of female physicians, midwives, nurses, and servants to care for them (Dişli, 2021).

Furthermore, maristāns did little to restrict their beneficiaries (Ragab, 2015). In fact, they rarely imposed requirements for beneficiaries to be Muslim or non-Muslim, poor or wealthy, male or female, and resident or non-resident of the local city (Lev, 2005; Peters et al., 2012). However, disenfranchised populations were often prioritised (Altıntaş, 2022; Lev, 2005). For instance, in Haseki Dār al-Shifā', free medication in the outpatient clinic was a service reserved for those who could not afford to pay for their prescriptions otherwise (Ünver, 1939). Hence, we can assume that the healthcare system in maristāns was not designed to perpetuate an equity gap by marketing services to an already well-to-do upper class. Most maristāns, along with their corresponding waqfs, were purposefully created to serve those with limited access to treatment (Khan, 2015).

Operation of Maristāns: Organisation and Maintenance

Maristāns organised the tenets of operation through an endowment charter known as *waqfīyyah*. These documents provided information about the roles and expectations of the recruited staff, the hospital's income sources, and the management of generated revenue (Altıntaş, 2022; Sarı, 1995). The number of medical and ancillary personnel, the required skill set of each employee, the work ethic they would be expected to maintain, and the reasons for employment termination were also among the terms defined in *waqfīyyah* documents (Sarı, 1995; Taşkıran, 1972). They even articulated the sum allocated for specific expenses, such as the staff's salary and kitchen costs (Altıntaş, 2022; Günay, 2012).

The administrative hierarchy of the maristān system placed significant importance on the chief physician. The chief physician was in charge of the medical supervision of patients and the day-to-day maintenance of the hospital (Sarı, 1995). Attending physicians examined patients regularly during their stay (Sarı, 2020). In some maristāns, the examination occurred twice a day; in other accounts, it was twice a week (Lev, 2005; Sarı, 2020). When the mediaeval French traveller Jean-Baptiste Tavernier (d. 1689 CE) wrote his observations from the Enderun hospital in Istanbul—the infirmary stationed inside the royal palace of the Sultan—he noted with surprise that the hospital was organised and well-maintained. In his travel account, Tavernier writes:

> The two principal physicians and the two principal surgeons...make their visits there every day at certain hours. A man cannot imagine a place better ordered and regulated than this: and the Grand Seignior [Sultan] himself sometimes comes there in person to take an exact account of the sick and their condition, as also to enquire whether they are well treated, whether the physicians visit them often and whether every officer of the infirmary performs the duty incumbent on him. Tavernier (1684, p. 20)

The introduction of individualised patient records by the chief physician and founder of a maristān in Baghdad, Abū Bakr Muḥammad ibn Zakariyyā' al-Rāzī (d. 925 CE), also informed and contextualised treatment in maristāns. Such records contributed to the administrative efficiency and accuracy of maristān institutions and often included patient information such as age, sex, profession, and medical history (Adamson, 2017; Al-Ghazal, 2007).

The waqf founder would also select a trustee to manage the financial affairs of the operating institution and all attached properties included in the waqf (Günay, 2012). Trustees, called *nāthir, mutawallī*, or *qayyim*, were tasked with protecting the endowment, managing its resources in alignment with the *waqfīyyah*, and ensuring the proper maintenance of services (Günay, 2012; Peters et al., 2012). As such, they were expected to maintain an acceptable ratio of income to spending and to prioritise covering costs as outlined in the waqf deed. Any surplus funds were to be distributed according to the philanthropic preferences of the sponsor (Lev, 2005). Trustees were also responsible for non-specialised staff assignments, payment of staff salary, and overall supervision of the hospital's operations (Altıntaş,

2022). The disposition of a trustee was allowed as long as it did not corrupt the waqf's mission. A system of checks and balances existed to account for cases when a trustee would deviate against the founder's will or the original endowment. The trustee's decisions could be investigated, altered, or nullified in these cases. For instance, if a trustee approved an overpriced purchase or renovation project for the hospital, their decision could be overturned by judges to ensure that the financial resources of the waqf were not exploited (Ansari, 2013).

Thus, the trustee's authority over the maristān's financial affairs was mirrored by the chief physician's authority regarding the maristān's medical affairs. These positions would occasionally overlap, as demonstrated in the following quotation from the son of court physician Sinān ibn Thābit (d. 943 CE), who served under Abbasid caliph al-Muqtadir:

> [In] the year 306 AH (June, 918 CE), my father inaugurated Bīmaristān al-Sayyidah in Sūq Yaḥya (a neighbourhood in Baghdad). He sat there, arranged the physicians [in shifts], and admitted patients. He built it overlooking the Tigris, and its expenditure was six hundred dinars a month. In this year as well, my father…established [a bīmaristān] at the Gate of the Levant and named it al-Bīmaristān al-Muqtadirī, and spent on it [from the caliph's] money two hundred dinars a month. (Thābit ibn Sinān, as quoted by Ragab, 2015, p. 38)

The interdisciplinary pillars of the maristān administrative system also included judicial and political figures to augment stability (Bayartan, 2008; Günay, 2012). Such professionals were authorised in the *waqfīyyah* to inspect the operation of waqfs. For example, due to reported complaints regarding the al-ʿAḍudī Hospital in Baghdad, the caliph's court prompted an investigation to determine whether the hospital's medicinal purchases aligned with inpatient needs (Lev, 2005). It was not uncommon for government-appointed judges to supervise the management of waqf-affiliated properties and contracts to the extent that any change or adjustment would require legal authorisation (Günay, 2012; Lev, 2005). *Qāḍī's* would oversee the endowments in their respective locale through various methods (Bayartan, 2008): the verification of a waqf's legal tenets, the abolition of inactive waqfs, the transfer from existing waqf properties to new sources of income, and the mobilisation of resources between different endowed charities based on the changing needs of the institutions (Akgündüz, 2000; Lev, 2005). Thus, legal authorities offered endowed charities protection from misuse and abuse through their close surveillance (Günay, 2012). In summary, a diverse group of representatives that comprised founders, trustees, legal and medical authorities, and state agencies controlled the finance, administration, and maintenance of waqf institutions (Lev, 2005).

Medical Practitioners of Maristāns

Physicians undoubtedly led the medical operations of maristāns. *Waqfīyyah* documents repeatedly mention scrupulous management skills, attentiveness during patient check-ups, and compassion towards patients among the professional requirements for maristān physicians (Hunke, 1997; Sarı, 1995, 2020). The number of physicians in circulation usually corresponded with the scale of each maristān. For instance, al-ʿAḍudī Hospital, which was recognised as one of the most magnificent hospitals in the mediaeval period, reportedly employed twenty-four physicians (Hamarneh, 1962; Lev, 2005). They were generally assigned by higher bureaucratic officials or endowment supervisors and were paid well for their time (Hamarneh, 1962; Ünver, 1939). Physicians would travel great distances to join the medical teams of famous maristāns (Hamarneh, 1962). For example, al-Dakhwār (d. 1230 CE)—the teacher of many renowned Muslim physicians, including the physician and medical historian ibn Abī Uṣaybiʿah—built his career as a sought-after private practitioner based upon his practice at the Nūr al-Dīn Hospital in Damascus (Ali, 1996; Meyerhof & Schacht, 1968).

Physicians were supported by an interdisciplinary care team. Medical students, pharmacists, bloodletting experts, sick nurses, religious leaders similar to today's chaplains, and companions similar to today's social workers would accompany doctors on their rotational visits, retrieving and administering whatever medication or treatment modality the doctor ordered as they checked on each patient (Awaad et al., 2019; Issa, 1928). They operated via a shift system to keep patients under close observation and care throughout the day and night (Sarı, 1995; Taşkıran, 1972).

While there were certainly specialists (e.g., ophthalmologists, optometrists, orthopaedic doctors, and surgeons trained to treat wounds, tumours, hernias, and infections), hospital physicians were most commonly polymaths dealing with a wide range of illnesses, among which was mental illness (Yıldırım & Altungök, 2015). As mentioned in the *waqfīyyah* of the Haseki Dār al-Shifā', it was part of the physician's job to discern patients' personalities, temperaments, and dispositions (Taşkıran, 1972; Ünver, 1939). This analytical competency was pertinent to the efficacy of mental healthcare offered in maristāns.

Becoming a physician necessitated an advanced understanding of pharmacology (Sarı, 2020; Ünver, 1939). Historical sources state that physicians often prepared medications themselves. In other cases, a pharmacist would prepare and stock medications (Hamarneh, 1962). The hospital pharmacies enforced drug purity regulations and prioritised high standards for the quality, freshness, and measurement of medicinal ingredients (Alotaibi, 2021; Sarı, 2020). The distribution and administration of medicines from the pharmacy often required approval from the chief physician in the maristān (Issa, 1928). In cases where the quality of the medication was called into question, judges exercised the authority to inspect maristāns and hold staff accountable for improper pharmacological practice (Sarı, 2020). In describing ibn Ṭūlūn's maristān in Cairo, 10th-century chronicler al-Balawī writes:

> [Ibn Ṭūlūn's] piety was evident with great enthusiasm and proper intentions; [as in his] building the mosque and the bīmaristān, [which] included, in its drug cabinets, the most precious and effective drugs, and well-known theriacs, which are only [found] in the drug cabinets of kings and caliphs. His bīmāristān was never missing any of the medications or the major drugs, such as the musk treatment and others... He bought for [the bīmaristān] precious revenues, [only] some of which would suffice for all the needs [of the bīmaristān], should God protect whoever is administering them. (Ragab, 2015, p. 35)

Hospitals purchased a wide variety of substances derived from plants, animals, and minerals for pharmaceutical usage (Sarı 1995, 2020). Pharmacists and physicians traditionally synthesised medicines in the *shrabkhana* (pharmacy unit of hospitals) under the supervision of an assigned chief (Dashti, 2020). An account of the Qalāwūn Hospital in Cairo described imports from other parts of Egypt, Funjistan, Abyssinia, and, in reference to the Ruwenzori mountain range, 'mountains of the moon' (Dols, 1992, p. 124). These units provided medications for the inpatient wards and extended their services to the public during particular times of the week (Bakır & Başağaoğlu, 2009).

Medical Training in Maristāns

In maristāns, physicians were trained, tested, and evaluated in order to be deemed competent to practise medicine independently (Yıldırım & Altungök, 2015). Numerous maristāns had a functioning medical school attached to the hospital building, while others operated as training centres (Benli, 2016; Miller, 2006; Syed, 1981). Some records report physicians evaluating their students' performance by observing them in practice with patients (Issa, 1928). Qualifying for a medical education or a private apprenticeship at one of these maristāns was a challenging feat. Students would be selected carefully among those who had already completed their foundational *madrasah* education, formally covering the fields of Islāmic studies and the natural sciences (Ayduz, 2007). Once enrolled, students' medical education and accommodation were often fully sponsored (Khan, 2015).

These higher-education institutions were considered prestigious, financed generously by the hospitals' patrons, and furnished with extensive book collections (Pérez et al., 2012). As a result of their training, graduating physicians were expected to exhibit a high level of expertise that merged theoretical medicine with successful clinical practice (Sarı, 1995; Syed, 1981).

Licensure of Maristān Physicians and Litigation

Another significant characteristic of pre-modern Islāmicate medical practice was the establishment of licensure for physicians by the court physician Sinān ibn Thābit in 931 CE Baghdad under the authority of Abbasid Caliph al-Muqtadir (d. 932 CE; Ibn Abī Uṣaybiʿah, 1245–1246/2020; Syed, 1981). Since licences were only given by the *muḥtasib* (appointed market inspector), accreditation allowed patients to distinguish qualified physicians from charlatans and ensure the authenticity of their prescriptions (Al-Gharbi, 2021; Yassine, 2020). Physicians without a licence could be charged with administering fake medicines made from false materials like dyed starch and glue and were thus no longer trusted (Issa, 1928). Trainees also successfully completed a thesis and medical examination before being licensed as independent medical practitioners (Yıldırım & Altıngörk, 2015).

There were additional checks and balances to hold physicians accountable. If a patient died while receiving treatment in a maristān, the deceased's family could complain to the judicial court and request a consultation with a higher medical authority (Tschanz, 2017). The court would then collect the patient's prescription as evidence to evaluate the attending physician's diagnosis and treatment. We can infer that such measures empowered patients to insist on their right to receive care from a competent physician responsible for preserving health and life to the best of their ability.

Research, Peer Review, and Continued Education in Maristāns

Physicians were significant stakeholders within the waqf system, both endowing and working within maristāns and medical schools (Issa, 1928). Sometimes, without compensation, physicians would treat indigent patients within maristāns and serve as professors and supervisors for medical students (Al-Gharbi, 2021). For instance, the physician Kamel Eddine al-Hamsī (d. 615 CE) volunteered in the Nūr al-Dīn Maristān for years without being paid (Ibn Abī Uṣaybiʿah, 1245–1246/2020). Many physicians would also convert parts of their homes into classrooms. For example, al-Dakhwār endowed his house, library, and clinic to the Qalāwūn Maristān where the public was free to observe the peer review of medical studies and research (Ali, 1996; Ibn-an-Nafīs, 1968).

Various other records reveal a rich network of research materials, including collections of case studies and experiments that students could review and build upon with their own experiences. is al-Rāzī's (d. 925 CE) *Kitāb al-Ḥāwī fī al-Ṭibb* (The Comprehensive Book on Medicine), a 23-volumebook that detailed over 900 patient cases (Awaad et al., 2022; Tibi, 2006). The expertise of past physicians was also compiled, chronicled, and disseminated for study. For example, ibn Abī-Uṣaybiʿah compiled a biographical encyclopaedia of over 430 physicians leading up to his time (Ibn Abī Uṣaybiʿah, 1245–1246/2020). In one of his accounts, ibn Abī-Uṣaybiʿah writes about the physician Abū al-Majd ibn Abī al-Ḥakam (d. 1174 CE), who worked in the Nūr al-Dīn maristān of Damascus:

> [He] used to examine the patients at the hospital, take note of their condition and listen to their complaints in the presence of the nurses and porters, who were charged with looking after them. All methods of treatment and prescriptions he gave were included in the letter. After finishing his ward round, he would pass on to a magnificently furnished hall to consult there various scientific works...There, all physicians and students gathered around him in order to discuss medical points. When he had asked questions of his pupils and worked for about three hours in the wards and in the library, he would return to his home. (Elgood, 2010, p. 237)

Endowment documents from Ottoman hospitals would also request the attendance of physicians for regular consultation assemblies to discuss cases with peers and call on the opinion of higher medical authorities (Sarı, 2020). Prominent physician Abbās Wasīm Efendi (d. 1760) even advised his colleagues to improve their medical expertise by deliberately serving in maristāns, which allowed them to see a wide range of rare diseases (Sarı, 2020). Thus, the evidence-based approach to medical practice during the height of Islāmicate civilisation flourished through the exchange and critique of case studies, clinical trials, and medical writings (Awaad et al., 2019).

Administrative and Ancillary Personnel of Maristāns

In addition to the physicians, pharmacists, nurses, and medical students that made up the medical department, each section of the maristān employed section-specific staff and supervisors (Issa, 1928). Staff numbers fluctuated depending on the financial capacity of the institution and the density of need among its assigned population. For example, Ottoman dār al-shifā's had an average staff of twenty-four individuals (Altıntaş, 2022). The 16th-century Haseki Dār al-Shifā' in Istanbul employed a team of twenty-eight people, which is a relatively large number considering the hospital's limited capacity for admitting patients (Taşkıran, 1972); thus, the ratio of provider to patient was relatively high (Sarı, 1995).

Hospitals were known to make ancillary recruitments depending on the needs of the patients. These employees included *mu'adhdhin* (caller to prayer), imams, and spiritual advisors (akin to chaplains today); security guards, clerks, stewards/butlers, pantrymen, cleaners, sanitation workers, and laundry workers; incense burners, bath attendants, cooks, and gardeners, among other positions (Awaad et al., 2019; Hamarneh, 1962; Lev, 2005; Sarı,

1995; Taşkıran, 1972; Ünver, 1939). Some hospitals also employed musicians to deliver therapeutic performances to patients as part of the treatment process (Erer & Atıcı, 2010). Religious sources of support were offered, but not mandated, to those who sought them, and mentally ill patients were rarely dismissed as morally corrupt or religiously deficient (Dols, 1992; Pérez et al., 2012; Scalenghe, 2014)

Special attention was paid to the kitchen because patients' diets constituted an essential component of the treatment plan (Hamarneh, 1962; McClary, 2021). In many hospitals, food was prepared onsite, while in other cases, there were soup kitchens within the larger endowed complex that would provide meals for the patients and staff. The pantryman, cook, and şerbetî (one who prepares drinks and syrups) were among the employees in charge of dietary services (Taşkıran, 1972). Historical sources document the careful preparation of food (Sarı, 2008, 2020) that aligned with the patient's prescription and the standards spelt out in *waqfīyyah* documents (Sarı, 2020).

Administrative and ancillary personnel allowed maristāns to operate internally as an autonomous institution (Altıntaş, 2022; Taşkıran, 1972). We see the effects of this in the organisation and implementation of high-quality patient diets, the maintenance of clean indoor and outdoor hospital wards, and the assured security of patients while under hospital supervision (Hamarneh, 1962).

Conclusion

The waqf system facilitated a culture of charitable endowments whose endurance manifested in the establishment and maintenance of maristāns. These waqfs prioritised self-sustaining sources of income that were elastic enough to adapt to a constantly evolving economy and world. The administrative pillars on which these maristāns were established allowed them to use their endowed waqfs to provide high-quality treatment to society's most vulnerable populations over the course of centuries. The administration and maintenance of these hospitals relied on multiple medical, judicial, and financial stakeholders to ensure a healthy distribution of responsibilities and an integrated system of checks and balances by which the charitable intention of the maristān was preserved.

The sponsorship of healthcare for all beneficiaries of maristāns applied to all (waqf deed of Qalāwūn Maristān c. 1284 CE as cited by Tschanz, 2017). Such a vision reflected the medical ideals throughout the classical Islāmicate world. At the same time, it is essential to note that the organisation and administration of maristāns varied between geographical regions and time periods as our scope is cast over quite a large expanse of space and time (Hamarneh, 1962). However, identifying the mechanics behind cases where successful maristāns indeed fulfilled these ideals can offer valuable insights. We cannot consider a revival of Muslim mental healthcare without first scrutinising and reforming the financial inequities that pervade our societies today. While the context of mediaeval Islāmic societies differs significantly from modern nations, there exists a common vision for more cost-effective, all-inclusive, holistic mental health services.

References

Adamson, P. (2016). Abū Bakr al-Rāzī (d. 925), the spiritual medicine. In K. El-Rouayheb & S. Schmidtke (Eds.), *The Oxford Handbook of Islamic Philosophy* (pp. 63–82). Oxford University Press.

Ahmed, H. (2007). *Waqf-Based Microfinance: Realizing the Social Role of Islamic Finance*. World Bank.

Akgündüz. (2000). *TDV İslâm Ansiklopedisi*. irşādī Vakif. https://islamansiklopedisi.org.tr/irşādī-vakif

Akman, A. (2020). Vakıf medeniyetimizde Darüşşifalar. *In Koronavirüs döneminde güncel hukuki meseleler sempozyumu*, Bildiri Tam Metin Kitabı 29–30 Mayıs 2020. https://openaccess.ihu.edu.tr/xmlui/bitstream/handle/20.500.12154/1234/sempozyum11.pdf?sequence=1&isAllowed=y

Akyıldız, Y., & Abay, A. R. (2017). Vakıf müessesesinin gelişimi ve mahiyeti tarihsel bir değerlendirme. *Yalova Sosyal Bilimler Dergisi*, 7(15), 141–157. https://dergipark.org.tr/en/download/article-file/395273

Al-Gharbi, M. (2021). *People of the Book: Empire and Social Science in the Islamic Commonwealth Period. Socius*, 7. https://doi.org/10.1177/23780231211021200

Al-Ghazal, S. K. (2007). The origin of Bimaristans (hospitals) in Islamic medical history. *Foundation for Science Technology and Civilisation*, 1–10. https://muslimheritage.com/uploads/The_Origin_of_Bimaristans_%20in_Islamic_Medical_History.pdf

Ali, A. (1996). *Islamic Dynasties of the Arab East: State and Civilization During the Later Medieval* Times, M.D. Publications Pvt. Ltd.

Alotaibi, H. H. (2021). A review on the development of healthcare infrastructure through the history of Islamic Civilization. *Journal of Healthcare Leadership, Volume 13*, 139–145. https://doi.org/10.2147/jhl.s315323

Altıntaş, A. (2022). Andolu Tibbi Nedir-Neden Önemlidir? *Anadolu Tıbbı Dergisi*, *1*(1), 1. https://dergipark.org.tr/en/pub/anadolutibbi/issue/73485/1207955

Ansari, M. A. (2013). *Bīmāristāns and Waqf In Islam: Case Studies of Hospital Endowment during 9th to 13th Century CE in the Muslim World*. https://www.academia.edu/6955050/B%C4%ABm%C4%81rist%C4%81ns_and_Waqf_In_Islam_Case_Studies_of_Hospital_Endowment_during_9th_to_13th_Century_CE_in_the_Muslim_World

Ataseven, D. A. (1985). *Tarihimizde Vakfedilmiş Sağlık Müesseseleri "Darü'ş-şifalar"*, 6. https://acikerisim.fsm.edu.tr/xmlui/bitstream/handle/11352/628/Ataseven.pdf?sequence=1

Awaad, R., Mohammad, A., Elzamzamy, K., Fereydooni, S., & Gamar, M. (2019). Mental health in the Islamic golden era: The historical roots of modern psychiatry. *Islamophobia and Psychiatry: Recognition, Prevention, and Treatment*, 3–17. https://doi.org/10.1007/978-3-030-00512-2_1

Ayduz, S. (2007). Süleymaniye Medical Madrasa (Dār al-Tib) in the history of Ottoman medicine. *Foundation for Science Technology and Civilisation, 665*. https://www.muslimheritage.com/uploads/Suleymaniye_Medical_Madrasah.pdf

Bakir, B., & Basagaoglu, I. (2009). The Effects of the medical functions on architecture in Süleymaniye Dar'üş Şifa of the Ottoman Dar'üş Şifa. *Bulletin of the Transilvania*

University of Brasov. Medical Sciences. Series VI, 6, 71. http://webbut2.unitbv.ro/BU2009/BULETIN2009/SuplimentBU2009/pdf/13_Bakir.pdf

Bayartan, M. (2008). Osmanlı şehirlerinde vakıflar ve vakıf sisteminin şehre kattığı değerler. *Osmanlı Bilimi Araştırmaları, 10*(1), 157–175. https://dergipark.org.tr/en/download/article-file/13218

Benli, G. (2016). Hospitals in the Ottoman period and the work of Sinan the architect: Suleymaniye complex dar al-Shifa and the Medical Madrasa. *A+ Arch Design International Journal of Architecture and Design*, *2*(3), 1–9. https://dergipark.org.tr/en/pub/aarch/issue/42329/509301

Calder, N., & Hooker, M. B. (2012). Sharīʿa. *Encyclopaedia of Islam* (2nd ed.). https://referenceworks.brillonline.com/entries/encyclopaedia-of-islam-2/sharia-COM_1040

Dashti, R. (2020). Investigating the structure and organization of hospitals in Islamic civilization: From the middle of the second century to the middle of the eighth century AH. *IJMEHM*, *13*, 75–90. https://doi.org/https://ijme.tums.ac.ir/article-1-6224-en.html

Demir, A. (2019). *Selçuklu Dönemi Vakıflarında Kadınların Yeri, Divriği Ulu Camii ve Darüşşifası Örneği.pdf*. Vakıflar Genel Müdürlüğü Yayınları.

Dişli, G. (2015). Planning of functional spaces in ottoman-period hospitals (Darüşşifa) of Anatolia. *Al-Masāq*, *27*(3), 253–276.

Dişli, G. (2021). An analysis of gendering of space in historical hospitals of Anatolia. *Journal for Women's Studies*, *22*(1), 1–24. https://doi.org/10.33831/jws.v22i1.95

Dols, M. (1984). Insanity in byzantine and Islamic medicine. *Dumbarton Oaks Papers*, *38*, 135–148. https://doi.org/10.2307/1291501

Dols, M. W. (1992). *Majnūn: The Madman in Medieval Islamic Society*. Clarendon Press.

Elgood, C. (2010). A Medical History of Persia and the Eastern Caliphate: from the earliest times until the year AD 1932. Cambridge University Press.

Erer, S., & Atıcı, E. (2010). Selçuklu ve Osmanlılarda Müzikle Tedavi Yapılan Hastaneler. *36*(1), 29–32. https://dergipark.org.tr/en/pub/uutfd/issue/35281/391528

Günay, H. M. (2012). *TDV İslam Ansiklopedisi*. Vakif - TDV İslâm Ansiklopedisi. https://islamansiklopedisi.org.tr/vakif

Hamarneh, S. (1962). Development of hospitals in Islam. *Journal of the History of Medicine and Allied Sciences*, *XVII*(3), 366–384. https://doi.org/10.1093/jhmas/XVII.3.366

Hunke, S. (1997). *Le Soleil d'Allāh brille sur l'Occident*. Albin Michel

Ibn Abī Usaybi'ah, M. (1995). *Uyūn al-Anbā' fī Tabaqāt al-Aṭibbā'*. Dar Maktabat Al Hayat.

Ibn Abī Uṣaybiʿah, M. (2020). *'Uyūn al-Anbā' fī Ṭabaqāt al-Aṭibbā'* [Best Accounts in the Classes of Physicians]. In E. Savage-Smith, S. Smith, & G. J. van Gelder (Trans.), *A Literary History of Medicine* (Vol. 134, Ser. *Handbook of Oriental Studies*. Section 1 *The Near and Middle East*). Brill. (Original work published 1245–1246 CE) https://doi.org/10.1163/37704_0668IbnAbiUsaibia.Tabaqatalatibba.lhom-tr-eng1

Ibn-an-Nafīs, 'AlīAIbn-al-Ḥazm, Meyerhof, M., & Schacht, J. (1968). *The theologus autodidactus of Ibn al-Nafīs*. Clarendon Press.

Issa, A. (1928). -كتاب تاريخ البيمارستانات في الإسلام. ص87- كتاب تاريخ البيمارستانات في الإسلام مارستان قلاوون [History of Bimaristāns in Islam]. https://shamela.ws/book/36083/85

Keshavarzi, H., & Ali, B. (2019). Islamic Perspectives on Psychological and Spiritual Well-Being and Treatment. In: Moffic, H., Peteet, J., Hankir, A., Awaad, R. (eds)

Islamophobia and Psychiatry: Recognition, Prevention, and Treatment (pp. 41–53). Springer.

Khan, M. T. (2015). Historical role of Islamic Waqf in poverty reduction in Muslim society. *The Pakistan Development Review*, *54*(4), 979–996. https://www.jstor.org/stable/43831378

Kök, B. (2007). *Nûreddin Zengî, Mahmud*. TDV İslâm Ansiklopedisi. https://islamansiklopedisi.org.tr/nureddin-zengi-mahmud

Lev, Y. (2005). *Charity, Endowments, and Charitable Institutions in Medieval Islam*. University Press of Florida. https://library.lol/main/56561F8BBEB3C3519E8E43DC738554B9

McClary, R. P. (2021). Dar al-shifa'or Bimaristān? Medieval Islamic hospitals of Damascus, Sivas and Cairo in the 12th and 13th Centuries. In M. Gharipour (Ed.), *Health and Architecture: The History of Spaces of Healing and Care in the Pre-Modern Era* (pp. 99–115). Bloomsbury Publishing.

Meyerhof, M., Schacht, J. (1968). *The Theologus Autodidactus of ibn al-Nafīs*. Clarendon Publications.

Miller, A. C. (2006). Jundi-Shapur, bimaristāns, and the rise of academic medical centres. *Journal of the Royal Society of Medicine*, *99*(12), 615–617.

Necipoğlu, G. (2013). *Sinan Çağı: Osmanlı İmparatorluğu'nda mimarî kültür*. İstanbul Bilgi Üniversitesi Yayınları.

Pérez, J., Baldessarini, R. J., Undurraga, J., & Sánchez-Moreno, J. (2012). Origins of psychiatric hospitalization in medieval Spain. *Psychiatric Quarterly*, *83*, 419–430.

Peters, R., Abouseif, D. B., Powers, D. S., Carmona, A., Layish, A., Lambton, A. K. S., Deguilhem, R., McChesney, R. D., Kozlowski, G. C., Hooker, M. B., & Hunwick, J. O. (2012). *Encyclopaedia of Islam* (2nd ed.).Waḳf. https://referenceworks.brillonline.com/entries/encyclopaedia-of-islam-2/wakf-COM_1333

Ragab, A. (2015). *The Medieval Islamic Hospital: Medicine, Religion, and Charity*. Cambridge University Press. https://doi.org/10.1017/CBO9781316271797

Sahih Muslim, (n.d.). *What Reward Reaches A Man After His Death*. sunnah.com - sayings and teachings of Prophet Muḥammad (ﷺ) https://sunnah.com/muslim:1631

Sarı, N. (1995). *Osmanlı Darüşşifalarına Tayin Edilecek Görevlilerde Aranan Nitelikler*. 11–54. https://www.academia.edu/47132902/Osmanl%C4%B1_Dar%C3%BC%C5%9F%C5%9Fifalar%C4%B1na_Tayin_Edilecek_G%C3%B6revlilerde_Aranan_Nitelikler

Sarı, N. (2008). *Ottoman Medical Practice and the Medical Science*. https://www.academia.edu/48969258/Ottoman_Medical_Practice_and_the_Medical_Science

Sarı, N. (2016). A review of Ottoman court records on mental diseases. *Journal of Health Culture*, *1*(1), 58–67.

Sarı, N. (2020, January 1). *Osmanlı Darüşşifasında Tedavi. In Afyon and Istanbul International Turkish-Islamic Medical History and Ethics Congresses (*2018–2019*) Proceedings Book*, Konya. https://www.academia.edu/46571791/Osmanl%C4%B1_Dar%C3%BC%C5%9F%C5%9Fifas%C4%B1nda_Tedavi

Scalenghe, S. (2014). *Disability in the Ottoman Arab World, 1500–1800: Cambridge Studies in Islamic Civilization*. Cambridge University Press. doi:10.1017/CBO9781107045309

Şentürk, M. (2010). *Vakif Kültürünün Kur'ân'daki Referanslari*. https://dergipark.org.tr/tr/download/article-file/260856

Surty, M. I. H. I. (1997, May 22). The Impact of the Shari'ah on the Development of Bimäristän in Muslim World-7th to 13th Century.pdf. International Conference of Islamic Medicine.

Syed, I. B. (1981). Islamic medicine: 1000 Years Ahead of its times. *Journal of the Islamic Medical Association of North America*, *13*(1). https://doi.org/10.5915/13-1-11925

Taşkıran, N. (1972). *Hasekinin Kitabı: İstanbul Haseki Külliyesi.pdf.* Yenilik Basımevi.

Tavernier, J. B. (1684). *Six voyages de Jean-Baptiste Tavernier.* (Vol. 1). Moses Pitt at the Angel in St. Pauls Church-yard.

Tibi S. (2006). Al-Razi and Islamic medicine in the 9th century. *Journal of the Royal Society of Medicine*, *99*(4), 206–207. https://doi.org/10.1177/014107680609900425

Tschanz, D. W. (2017, March). *The Islamic roots of the Modern Hospital.* AramcoWorld. https://www.aramcoworld.com/Articles/March-2017/The-Islamic-Roots-of-the-Modern-Hospital

Ünver, S. A. (1939). *400. Yıldönümü Dolayısıyla Haseki Hastanesi Tarihçesi.* Kader Basımevi.

Yassine, R. (2020). The Role of Islamic Civilization in the Evolution and Development of Medical Thinking. Doctoral dissertation, Sidi Mohamed Ben Abdellah University Morocco. https://cdim.fmp-usmba.ac.ma/mediatheque/e_theses/157-20.pdf

Yıldırım, T., & Altungök, A. (2015). Abbasiler Döneminde İslam Tıbbı ve Toplum Sağlığı. *Fırat Üniversitesi Sosyal Bilimler Dergisi*, *25*(2), Article 2. https://doi.org/10.18069/fusbed.03936

4 Cure and Care

A Survey of Diagnosis and Treatment of Mental Illness in Maristāns

Salma Albezreh and Merve Nursoy-Demir

Introduction

Islāmicate medicine interprets contemporary evidence-based medical conventions through the religious framework established by Islāmic primary sources (Qur'ān and Ḥadīth) in order to apply a God-centred approach to healing (Sanitis, 2012). This intellectually rich and diverse tradition developed as a cumulative science under numerous Muslim dynasties and is arguably still being carved out today (Nagamia, 2003). From the rise of the Abbasid Caliphate in the 8th century to the waning of the Ottoman Empire in the 19th century, maristāns institutionalised the teaching and practising of Islāmicate medicine (Awaad et al., 2022). Muslim scholarship not only inherited preceding medical, pharmacological, and pharmaceutical traditions (e.g., Hippocratic, Galenic, Syriac, Persian, Indian, and Chinese) but also developed its own traditions with distinct and innovative methodologies (Nagamia, 2003; Nasr & De Santillana, 1968; Sarı et al., 2003).

Islāmicate medicine was not a static, homogeneous field. Instead, it consisted of multiple complementary medical traditions that permitted diverse and dynamic application across cultures and time periods (Murphey, 1992; Yüksel-Özkaya, 2016). For instance, the medicine practised in hospitals was principally inspired by Ancient Greek medicine, while folkloric and Prophetic medical traditions coexisted as complementary subsystems of healing in either private practice or under the domain of spiritual community centres, often known as Sufi lodges (Shefer-Mossensohn, 2009; Tunaboylu-Ikiz, 1999). Hence, a multi-disciplinary approach to health and wellness characterised many pre-modern Muslim communities due to the conjoined nature of *madāris* (schools for Islāmic learning), medical schools, spiritual community centres, and hospitals (Şengül, 2015).

This chapter surveys over 1,000 years of Islāmicate medicine as it was theorised, taught, and practised in and adjacent to pre-modern Muslim hospitals. More specifically, we introduce the foundational influence of the humoral and bio-psycho-social-spiritual frameworks and survey the

DOI: 10.4324/9781003329589-4

methods of classification, diagnosis, treatment, and aftercare within maristāns. Importantly, our vast chronological and spatial scope is meant to highlight relevant treatments and curative patterns rather than unjustly suggest that the historical diversity of Islāmicate medical theory and practice can be reduced to a monolithic portrait. Through this method, we aim to situate the evolving theory of Islāmicate medicine as it pertains to mental health within its historical practice and extrapolate evidence-based examples to enrich discussions of a modern holistic model.

Focusing on the Foundation: Two Medical Frameworks Found in Pre-Modern Maristāns

Humoral Theory: The Medical Framework in Pre-Islāmic Practice

Galen of Pergamon's (d. 217 CE) humoral theory was the baseline from which pre-modern Islāmicate medical frameworks sprung forth (Nutton, 2006; Pérez et al., 2012). According to Galenic theory, health is determined by a balance of four bodily fluids and their associated temperament: blood (sanguine), yellow bile (choleric), black bile (melancholic), and phlegm (phlegmatic; Scalenghe, 2014). An individual's combination of humours (i.e., temperaments) can be assessed to determine their position on the spectrums of temperature (cold vs. hot) and humidity (dry vs. humid). Each of these humours is associated with one of the four elements of nature (air, fire, earth, water; Sarı, 2020), one of the four seasons (spring, summer, fall, winter), and one of the four vital organs (heart, liver, spleen, and brain; Scalenghe, 2014).

Disease could result from an imbalance in this particular amalgam, leading to the deterioration or metastasisation of some humours over others. For example, two pre-modern terms that denoted mental illness were melancholia and mania, the first of which was often characterised as cold and wet, while the second was considered hot (Singer, 2018). In order to diagnose and treat ailments using this framework, physicians were expected to be well-versed in pre-modern pharmacology, where medications and therapeutic interventions were understood to interact with the varying temperaments or mixtures (*mizāj*) of patients (Sarı, 1995).

Bio-Psycho-Social-Spiritual Framework of Mental Health

While Galen and his Greek contemporaries did discuss mental illness—often as a purely physiological phenomenon that could be traced to a particular part of the body (McDonald, 2014)—it was within a pre-Islāmic framework that was not holistic in nature (Singer, 2018). As early Muslim scholars translated, dissected, and reconfigured these pre-Islāmic works, many rejected Greek philosophy's dualistic approach to the mind and body (Modanlou,

2008) and linked their knowledge of the body with a field that continues to expand among scholars today: *Ilm al-Nafs* (Deuraseh & Abu Talib, 2005). Discussions of treatment went beyond maintaining the body's physical functions or reducing pain; they aspired to raise patients to their highest physical, intellectual, and spiritual potential, believing that each was a precursor for the other. It was this distinctly multi-disciplinary approach to understanding human ontology that set the IP tradition apart from previous or parallel medical traditions (Awaad et al., 2019).

Although the bio-psycho-social-spiritual model is discussed in contemporary literature as a modern humanistic framework (Saad, 2017), historical evidence suggests that it was this same holistic view that characterised the ideals of mental health treatment in maristāns. Some of the most compelling evidence for the bio-psycho-social-spiritual model comes from the self-propagating authorship of *Ilm al-Nafs* across professionally, geographically and chronologically diverse contexts. Medical works like al-Rāzī's (d. 925 CE) *Comprehensive Book of Medicine*, al-Balkhī's (d. 934 CE) *Sustenance of the Body and Soul*, al-Majūsī's (d. 994 CE) *The Royal Notebook*, ibn Sīnā's (Avicenna, d. 1037 CE) *Canon of Medicine*, and ibn al-'Ayn Zarbi's (d. 1153 CE) *Al-Kāfī fit-Ṭibb*, set new precedents for classifying and diagnosing symptoms of mental illness, identifying root causes, and administering appropriate interventions (Awaad & Ali, 2015; Awaad et al., 2019, 2022; Badri, 2013; Haque, 2004).

Beyond medical treatises, we find pioneers in philosophy such as al-Kindi (d. 870 CE), al-Farabī (d. 950 CE), ibn Miskawayh (d. 1030 CE), ibn Bājja (Avempace—d.1138 CE), ibn Rushd (Averroes—d. 1198 CE), and Mulla Sadra (d. 1641 CE) writing extensively on the psychology of the soul, mind, heart, and brain (Awaad et al., 2019; Haque, 2004). Further, al-Muḥāsibī (d. 857 CE), ibn Hazm (d. 1064 CE), and al-Ghazālī (d. 1111 CE) wrote about diseases rooted in moral, emotional, or spiritual states, assigning to each a pathology and treatment method with practical steps for disease management, self-improvement, and self-discipline (Awaad et al., 2019). This rich repository of literature demonstrates investment in mental wellness from multiple sectors of the pre-modern Islāmic society. Moreover, the preservation and exegesis of these works until today suggest that they likely informed and influenced maristān physicians (Haque, 2004).

Identifying Mental Illness in Maristāns

Classifications of Mental Illness: Patterns across Time

The historical ambiguity of the contours of mental illness was compounded by the fact that maristāns operated across languages, empires, and cultures (Canino & Alegría, 2008; Dols, 1992; Kirmayer & Young, 1999). Thus, there was no universal classification method for mental illnesses that all maristāns adhered to (Awaad et al., 2019). Some patterns emerge, however, from the medical manuscripts of prominent physicians and scholars who set precedents for the classification of mental illness in their respective times.

One example is that of ‘Alī ibn Sahl Rabbān al-Ṭabarī (d. 870 CE) in one of the first medical encyclopaedias, *Firdaws al-Ḥikmah* (*Paradise of Wisdom*). In his chapter on diseases of the brain, al-Ṭabarī identifies thirteen types of diseases that stem from the corruption of the brain or the stomach and abdomen. These ailments include *ṣar*ʿ (epilepsy), *waḥshā* (shyness or solitariness), *waswasah* (obsessions), *hadhayān* (delirium), *fasād al-khayāl wal ʿaql* (the corruption of the imagination and reason), *nasyān* (forgetfulness), *sahar* (insomnia), *subāt* (lethargy), *dawīī* (ringing in the ears), *dawwār* (vertigo), *waram* (swelling), and headaches (Ṭabarī, n.d.; Meyerhof, 1931). Following close behind, Abu Zayd al-Balkhī (d. 934 CE) classified the following: *al-ġhadab* (anger); *al-jaza*’ (sadness and depression); *al-faza*’ (fears and phobias); and *wasawes al-ṣadr* (obsessional disorders) in his book, *Treatise on Sustenance of the* Body and Soul (Badri, 2013). Within his chapter on obsessional disorders, al-Balkhī made the distinction between time and symptom-dependent obsessions. Within these categories, al-Balkhī analyses the chronological onset of obsessions and the types of affliction they cause (Badri, 2013; Awaad & Ali, 2015). Al-Balkhī’s student, al-Rāzī, further differentiated between mental disorders that exhibit ‘impaired perception with healthy thinking, impaired thinking with healthy perception, and concurrent impairment of perception and thinking’ (Tabatabaei & Jafari-Mehdiabad, 2020, p. 4; Awaad et al., 2022).

Five centuries later, 15th-century Ottoman physician Mukbilzade Mu’min categorised many psychiatric conditions as head diseases, which preserved al-Ṭabarī’s position from the 9th century (Sarı, 1986; Ṭabarī, n.d.). The overarching diagnosis was *sersam* (i.e., a head swell) with additional subtypes based on the predominant body humour that was linked to the disease. These diseases would be categorised today as neuropsychiatric conditions, which could include psychiatric symptoms (e.g., insomnia, dementia, agitation, madness, and confusion) that require behaviour-based interventions and neurological symptoms (e.g., slowness in movement, headaches, and drowsiness) that require somatic interventions (Awaad et al., 2019).

Patterns of distinction emerged based on additional criteria, one of them being permanence (Tabatabaei & Jafari-Mehdiabad, 2020). For example, some pre-modern physicians held that ‘*atāhah*, (i.e., ‘idiocy’ or cognitive disability) was chronic, as opposed to melancholia or madness (Scalenghe, 2014). There was also a distinction between impairments directly associated with spirituality, whose subjects were known as ‘holy fools’, and those that were not (Scalenghe, 2014). Additionally, some writers classified psychosomatic conditions, such as *hafakan* (anxiety) or *ihtinak-i rahm* (hysteria), under the categories of heart disease or stomach disease based on the organs of the body from which symptoms manifested (Sarı, 1986).

Some other independent categories of mental illnesses included addiction disorders (e.g., alcoholism, *afyonkeş* [opioid addiction], tobacco addiction), traumatic brain injury, and *infialat-i nefsaniye* (personality disorder; Sarı, 1986). *Nafkhae malikholia* (sexual impotence) and nightmares were other diagnosable conditions sometimes associated with psychological illness (Haque, 2004; Syed, 1981). The discernment between such a broad range of enigmatic conditions suggests that a significant amount of attention was paid to the pathology and symptomatology associated with each condition.

Methodologies for Diagnosing Mental Illness: A Contextualised Approach

In the absence of modern screening or laboratory testing tools, the investigative expertise of pre-modern physicians was essential for accurately recognising mental illnesses (Sarı, 2020). In addition to the apparent symptoms of the patient, maristān physicians collected physiological information through the following main channels: a detailed medical history taken from the patient; a physical examination conducted by the physician to inspect any discolouration of the face and eyes, the smell of urine, or the amount of saliva; and an examination of any disturbance in the biological rhythms of the pulse, heartbeat, and breath (Nasr, 1968; Sarı, 1986; 2020). Physicians also conducted an analysis on the makeup of a patient's blood to determine the humoral nature of the illness, a process that was often repeated to evaluate the effectiveness of treatment (Al-Majūsī, n.d.; Dols, 1992).

In addition to physical examinations, physicians took note of many psychological signs and symptoms of their patients. Interestingly, ibn Sīnā analysed the implicit feelings of patients by observing patients' involuntary fluctuations in pulse rate when confronted with different suggestions, a strategy also employed by al-Majūsī for diagnosing lovesickness and centuries later by Carl Jung (d. 1961 CE) as 'word-association tests' (Dols, 1992; Fierro, 2022; Syed, 1981). The patient's disposition, coherence of thought, irritability, and tone of stress, anger, or despondency also offered an insight into what mental illness they were suffering from (Al-Majūsī, n.d.; Scalenghe, 2014; Ṭabarī, n.d.). For example, al-Rāzī associated melancholia with pensive personalities as opposed to manic patients who exhibited unrelenting thoughts and more 'hot-blooded', restless, and aggressive behaviour (Awaad et al., 2022; Tabatabaei & Jafari-Mehdiabad, 2020).

Moreover, physicians considered environmental factors, including the climate, season, time of the year, how far along the patient was in their sickness, and other circumstances that may trigger an onset of psychological distress, such as bereavement (Badri, 2013; Al-Majūsī, n.d.; Sarı, 1982;

Scalenghe, 2014). Another differentiation was made based on how often the onset of illness would occur and whether the illness was constant or afflicted in episodes, as in the case of epilepsy (Dols, 1992). Patients' interactions with others, or lack thereof, informed the physician's diagnoses as well, often revealing suspicious or distrustful perceptions of others (Dols, 1992; Scalenghe, 2014). Al-Balkhī listed dysfunctional beliefs among the symptoms of obsessional disorders by which the patient could not perform daily tasks due to intrusive, irrational thoughts (Badri, 2013; Awaad & Ali, 2015). Furthermore, physicians recognised the variation in symptomology between men, women, children, and adults (Badri, 2013; Al-Majūsī, n.d.; Dols, 1992; Sarı, 1982).

Physicians in maristāns often alluded to the importance of diagnosing the pathological root of observed symptoms to avoid extraneous interventions. Specifically, much of the pre-modern literature suggests that psychological illness can cause some bodily manifestations of the disease and, conversely, psychological manifestations of illness can result from a bodily disease (Badri, 2013; Al-Gharbi, 2021; Dols, 1992). For example, al-Balkhī identifies the corporeal manifestations of a deficiency in anger management as unintelligible speech, discolouration, tremors, and increased blood flow and body temperature (Badri, 2013). He also warns that leaving fears, depression, and obsessions unaddressed could lead to severe physiological comorbidities (Badri, 2013). As another example, al-Majūsī discusses differences in treatments for melancholia if observed in concurrence with a disruption in a woman's menstrual cycle (Al-Majūsī, n.d.). He also discusses cases where anxiety, fear, insomnia, and lethargy are symptoms of melancholia, suggesting that some mental illnesses could be qualified as a symptom of another predominant mental illness (Al-Majūsī, n.d.; Dols, 1992).

Treatment Methods in Maristāns

The hospitalisation of mentally ill patients was often an impetus for recovery. Al-Rāzī went so far as to suggest that in cases of unremitting mania, hospitalisation was the most critical step (Tabatabaei, & Jafari-Mehdiabad, 2020). In al-Balkhī's *Treatise on Sustenance of the Body and Soul*, he establishes the importance of seeking professional treatment for mental illness instead of relying on oneself:

> ...[T]he benefit one obtains externally from advice and counselling is more useful than a person's internal attempt (at treatment) through generating his own therapeutic thoughts...In that he is like a physician who falls ill to the extent that he fails to diagnose and treat himself, needing another doctor to treat him.
>
> (Badri, 2013, p. 35)

He clarifies that internal practices of positive cognition must accompany treatment from physicians and clinicians, thus distributing the responsibility for a favourable prognosis between the provider and the patient (Badri, 2013). Court records capturing the testimonies of mentally ill patients (Sarı, 2016), along with records of physicians' manuscripts, pharmacology collections, and archived prescription notes (Sarı, 1982), echo this humanistic approach (Shefer-Mossensoh, 2009).

While the patient's attitude played an essential role in treatment efficacy, providers were still responsible for formulating an effective treatment plan. Prescriptions could include therapeutic diets, medications, music therapy, behavioural therapy, phlebotomy, massage therapy, and even cauterisation. Such interventions were then supplemented by exercise regimens and recommended activities such as outdoor exposure, baths, rest, singing, reading poetry, and conversation or storytelling (Al-Majūsī, n.d.; Awaad et al., 2019).

The degree of detail assigned to each mental illness and its taxonomy of compounded treatments is consistent throughout the pharmacological and pharmaceutical texts referenced in maristāns (Al-Majūsī, n.d.; Ṭabarī, n.d.; Nagamia, 2003). In a case of insomnia, for example, Ottoman physician Emir Çelebi (d. 1638–9 CE) would prescribe frequent baths, exposure to humidity, and sleep-inducing smells, as well as pouring heated *haşhaş* (opium poppy), violet flower, water lily, malt, and romaine lettuce water on the head with zucchini oil (Sarı, 1982). Physicians also demonstrated caution regarding side effects and took measures to avoid harming or disturbing the patient (Haque, 2004; Sarı, 2020). This intimate understanding of the patient's disposition led practitioners to utilise interventions minimally and carefully. Transitions were preferably gradual and prioritised restoring a healthy diet and circadian rhythm (Bahammam et al., 2018). The prominent Ottoman physician Abbas Vesim (d.1760 CE) suggested that physicians initiate their treatment plan with a non-invasive intervention, often a carefully formulated diet, before transitioning to medications. If these two were ineffective, other treatment tools, such as cauterisation or surgery, were to be considered (Sarı, 2020).

Diet

Medical texts employed in maristāns often included detailed accounts of food, its preparation, and its combination as an intervention for various conditions, including mental illness (Al-Majūsī, n.d.; Sarı, 2020). After all, food and medicine were often one and the same (Pitchon, 2016). Physicians' decisions regarding patient diets often allude to the Islāmic theme of balance (Shefer-Mossensohn, 2009). Sometimes, this entailed avoiding certain foods (Dols, 1992). For example, upon describing medications to treat insomnia, physician Emir Çelebi warns against consuming any food that is overly hot, sour, salty, or difficult to digest (Sarı, 1982). Melancholic patients, in particular, were to avoid foods that were theorised to increase the production of black bile—the widely suspected source of a melancholic disposition (Scalenghe, 2014).

Other times, prescriptions entailed increasing the consumption of specific foods, such as al-Majūsī's fruit-filled diet for melancholic patients (Al-Majūsī, n.d.). As a result, the maristān kitchen and its staff were essential. The cook crafted personalised, nutritious meals per the physician's prescription and the patient's temperament (Sarı, 2020). Even for patients whose treatment plans did not include a therapeutic diet, the hospitals routinely served complimentary meals of fresh meat, fruits, and vegetables (Awaad & Ali, 2015; Issa, 1928).

Medication

In cases where a diet did not sufficiently address the patient's illness, physicians turned to medicinal interventions. For example, al-Rāzī wrote in *Kitāb al-Ḥāwī*, 'If the physician can treat with nutrients, not medication, then he has succeeded. If, however, he must use medication, then it should be simple remedies and not compound ones' (Al-Rāzī, as cited by Tibi, 2006, p. 206). Al-Rāzī's contemporaries did not all necessarily agree with his criticism of polypharmacy and the issue of simple versus compound medications was debated by many different authors (Tibi, 2006).

Medication served as the primary treatment method used in maristāns, including for cases of psychiatric illness (Sarı, 1982). Some common medications used in maristāns for the mentally ill included diuretics, emetics, laxatives, expectorants, enemas, and sudorific drugs (Al-Majūsī, n.d.; Dols, 1992; Gorini, 2002; Meyerhof, 1935). Maristān clinicians often prescribed these medications to flush excessive bodily fluids out of the patient's system to restore humoral balance. We also see the regular usage of digestive and acid-reducing medications, as well as appetisers and tonics.

Some somatic treatments were prescribed in the form of ointments and creams, while others were consumed or inhaled as drinks, pills, buccal tablets, powders, electuaries, and herbal mixtures (Al-Majūsī, n.d.; Dols, 1992). Drugs were primarily vegetable-based, although animal and mineral-based drugs were also occasionally used (Gorini, 2007). Physicians employed analgesics, tranquillisers or sedatives, and somnific drugs to reduce pain, anxiety, and insomnia (Sarı, 2020; Ibn Abī Uṣaybiʿah, 1245–1246/2020). In psychiatric cases where a patient exhibited aggressive behaviour, sedatives like opium served as a tranquillising intervention (Abou-Saleh & Salloum, 2020; Gorini, 2002).

When doctors designed prescriptions, they reviewed dosage amounts, intervals, ingredients, and expiration dates (Al-Majūsī, n.d.; Kahl, 2007). They would consider the nature of substances (i.e., humidity and warmth based on the Galenic theory) in interaction with the particular temperament of the patient (Sarı, 2020). Until the 19th century, medications for inpatient and outpatient clinics were routinely prepared in maristāns to target a patient's particular set of symptoms.

Sound Therapy

Islāmicate medicine recognised an inherent relationship between melodic rhythms and biological rhythms such as pulse (Sarı, 2020). In cases where a defective pulse was detected, physicians could prescribe specific *maqāmāt* (tonal modes) to restore a healthy rhythm (Erer & Atıcı, 2010). The psychological effects of *maqāmāt* are discussed extensively in early Islāmicate medical texts, including those produced by well-known Ottoman head physicians Şuuri Hasan Efendi (d. 1693–1694 CE), Gevrekzâde Hasan Efendi (d. 1801 CE), and Dawud al-Antakī (d. 1599 CE; Ak, 2017; Gevrekzâde, 1794; Şuuri, 1677). Maristān physicians were strongly encouraged to extend their acquisition of tools to include skills in medicalised musical competence (Ak, 2017). Ottoman physician Gevrekzâde Hasan Efendi went so far as to claim that a physician's competency would be deficient for medical practice if it lacked a thorough familiarity with the effect of *maqāmāt* on the human body and soul (Gevrekzâde, 1794; Turabi, 2005). As a result, sound therapy developed into a characteristic element of maristāns.

Various sounds were purposefully integrated into maristāns, from natural sounds like water and bird songs to compositional music (Awaad & Nursoy-Demir, 2023). Maristān premises were also engineered with acoustics in mind, through which melodies could be effectively conveyed to patients (Erer & Atıcı, 2010). In his 17th-century travel account, Evliya Çelebi mentions that ten musicians with different instruments came to Bayezid Dār al-Shifā' three times a week to perform for patients. He describes in detail the featured *maqāmāt* and their apparently positive effects on psychiatric patients (Evliya Çelebi, 2006).

Numerous other eyewitness accounts describe how psychiatric patients enjoyed the regular performances of musicians in the maristān courtyards (Dols, 1992; Tavernier, 1684). Particular *maqāmāt* were selected based on each patient's psychiatric condition, such as tones that calmed aggressive patients and tones that elevated depressed patients (Kalender, 1987). There were also people known as *mu'nis al-ghurabā'* (entertainers of the strangers) who were required to softly recite the Qur'ān to soothe the sick (Daher, 2015). Examples of maristāns that offered medicalised sound therapy include Bayezid Dār al-Shifā' in Edirne, Suleymaniye and Fatih Dār al-Shifā's in Istanbul, Gevher Nesibe, Divriği Sultan Melik, and Amasya Dār al-Shifā's in Anatolia, Nūr al-Dīn and Arghun Bimaristāns in Syria, and the al-Mansūrī Bimaristān in Egypt (Erer & Atıcı, 2010; Shefer-Mossensohn, 2009).

Talk Therapies

In general, maristān physicians were advised to avoid talking with patients in a manner that could make them feel like an anomaly. The etiquette of provider-patient interactions was often outlined in maristān *waqfīyyah* (endowment charter) documents and included being attentive (Hunke, 1997; Sarı, 1995, 2020), soft-spoken, and upbeat (Ibn Abī Usaybi'ah, 1245–1246/2020). Furthermore, al-Rāzī established that a physician should always instil hope in their patients, even if the prognosis is uncertain (Ibn Abi Usaybi'a, 1245–1246/2020).

Many talk therapies utilised within maristāns aimed to reframe internal cognitions to eliminate negative thought patterns. In their counselling of psychiatry patients, physicians worked with patients to prepare cognitive tools to quell the onset of future negative thoughts and behaviours, emphasising mental hygiene (Badri, 2013; Awaad et al., 2019). For example, al-Rāzī recognised the potential for thoughts to facilitate or derail mental stability, and thus saw the provider as a critical force to counter faulty thinking and gently redirect patients to healthier, more sound cognitions—a practice we would now call cognitive reframing (Awaad et al., 2022; Tabatabaei & Jafari-Mehdiabad, 2020). Al-Rāzī operationalised this method by recommending that patients use a journal to externalise negative and irrational cognitions. Such practice-based tools helped to emphasise the importance of affirmation for building a positive self-image (Al-Gharbi, 2021; Awaad et al., 2019, 2022).

Complementary to al-Rāzī's emphasis on external and internal positive reinforcement was al-Balkhī's endorsement of external and internal therapy. His discussion on external therapy emphasised activities and social exercises to avoid amplifying obsessive thoughts, and internal therapy alluded to the historical equivalent of 'Insight Psychotherapy' (Awaad & Ali, 2015). Al-Balkhī encouraged individuals with obsessive thoughts to confide their fears in a trusted party that could help them distinguish between rational and irrational fears (Badri, 2013).

Another example that parallels modern practice is reciprocal inhibition, often written as *al-ʿilāj bi ḍid* (treatment with the opposite), in which a positive reward is associated with exposure to the individual's dreaded fear. This method was studied by al-Ghazālī and expounded upon by al-Balkhī to form what we would now call systematic desensitisation therapy (Badri, 2013). This method closely resembles exposure and response prevention (ERP), which is a form of cognitive behavioural therapy (CBT) used today to address phobias, obsessive-compulsive disorder (OCD), anxiety, and eating disorders (Hezel, 2019). Unique among his medical contemporaries, al-Balkhī approached phobias and obsessional disorders from a behavioural therapeutic approach in the form of *reyādat al-nafs* (training of the psyche; Awaad & Ali, 2016).

Furthermore, on regulating habits, ibn Miskawayh developed cycles of restraint, affirmation, reward, and punishment, or 'response cost', to develop productive habits and eliminate destructive ones (Al-Gharbi, 2021; Awaad et al., 2019; Haque, 2004). One unique application of this in maristāns was matching patients in the psychiatric ward with *murāfiqīn* (companions) to help sustain and encourage the patients' treatment regimen, self-care, and emotional wellness throughout the day, even after the physician rounded on them (Awaad et al., 2019).

Cauterisation

In maristāns, cauterisation (a medical procedure that entails the controlled application of heat, often with hot metal instruments or oils, to specific tissues or vessels) served as a tool to address many illnesses, including cases of psychiatric illness in which other interventions were ineffective (Sarı, 1988). In his book on surgery, 15th-century head physician of Amasya Dār al-Shifā' Şerafeddin Sabuncuoglu (d. 1468 CE) provides a detailed methodology to treat melancholia in which a metal cauterising tool is heated and applied to five points on the skull and the back of the head (Sarı, 1988). Interestingly, these points correspond with the points along the head and spine recognised by acupuncture experts today (Sarı, 1988).

Holistic and Integrated Treatment

Many features built into maristāns had underlying therapeutic functions, drawing from contemporary scientific research on how to improve patients' conditions. For example, the Arghun Maristān in Aleppo featured basil plants around a central fountain (Gorini, 2002), which can be attributed to the common belief that smells could reach the brain and improve its functioning (Gorini, 2007). Known to have antidepressant and tranquillising effects, the choice to plant basil demonstrates the intentionality with which the therapeutic spaces for mentally ill patients were designed.

Another typical example is baths or water therapy. A frequent recommendation in patients' treatment plans, the *ḥammām* was an essential component either within or adjacent to most maristān buildings. In cases where a hospital did not have a built-in *ḥammām*, the larger *kulliyah* offered bathing services. Special attention was given to the temperature and duration of baths and the aromatics that accompanied them (Gorini, 2007). Many treatment regimens called for hot baths in particular, presumably to counter the cold and dry humoral qualities associated with some mental illnesses (Dols, 1992).

Aside from hospital-wide structures, there is additional evidence that psychiatric patients were separated according to the severity of their mental illness and its manifestations (Dols, 1992). According to one account, some patients were restrained in cells while others were permitted to move freely (Pérez et al., 2012; Tudela, 1907). This may have been due to select patients' violent or erratic behaviour, considering the severity of their ailment prompted hospitalisation instead of home-bound care. In the interest of protecting the patients from themselves and others, more extensive measures were taken.

Discharge and Aftercare

Maristāns had convalescent wards dedicated to monitoring patients who were being cared for as they regained their strength before discharge (Ataseven, 1985; Yassine, 2020). The length of a patient's stay would depend on the severity and responsiveness of the patient's psychiatric illness (Ragab, 2015). In cases when a patient died under the supervision of the maristān, the hospital would offer an honourable burial with all expenses covered (Issa, 1928; Lev, 2005).

In Baghdad, Jewish traveller Benjamín de Tudela (d. 1173 CE) reported that the caliph would regularly send officials from the state to confirm the recovery of rehabilitated patients before having them discharged (Tudela, 1907; Pérez et al., 2012). Physicians would continue to visit their patients and congratulate them on their progress post-discharge (Ibn Abī Uṣaybiʿah, 1245–1246/2020). Sometimes, the hospital fashioned the discharged patient with a new complimentary *kiswa* (outfit), as observed in Qalāwūn Maristān in Cairo (Issa, 1928; Miller, 2006). Maristāns also offered psychiatric aftercare to discharged patients in the form of a stipend of gold dinars to make up for time spent out of the workforce, support their reintegration into society, and improve their chances of restoring a self-sustainable lifestyle (Ataseven, 1985; Awaad et al., 2022; Tudela, 1907). Such aftercare became a trademark of maristāns and the extension of concern for patients beyond the hospital walls (Awaad et al., 2022).

Conclusion

As an institution, the maristān served as a microcosm of the larger ecosystem of integrated ideas in ethics, healthcare, medicinal arts, and architecture, among other fields in the pre-modern Muslim world (Dashti, 2020; Shefer-Mossensohn, 2015). From a historical perspective, maristāns offered a unique lens through which we can better understand how research, technology, and medical advancements were deliberately directed to the forefront of the philanthropic landscape with profound consistency. This chapter also serves to highlight how the classification, diagnosis, and treatment of some psychological conditions are more historically consistent or stable than others. Such observations can serve to inform clinicians on how mental illness has been historically perceived and received by different traditions and cultures and how such historical precedents continue to influence help-seeking behaviour today.

In many ways, Islāmic medicine championed a polymathic practitioner who could balance multiple interventions from their prescriptive toolbox and practise exceptional dexterity in designing prescription plans (Haque, 2004). These treatment plans often incorporated bathhouses for water therapy, kitchens for therapeutic diets, pharmacies for medication, acoustic halls for sound therapy, herbs and florals for aromatherapy, and fountains and greenery to induce a sense of calm for agitated patients (Syed, 1981). The humanistic, multi-axial treatment plans that emerged from the maristān complexes served to exemplify the mind-body-soul connection that so clearly characterised the Islāmic psychological heritage of the Muslims (Awaad et al., 2022).

References

Abou-Saleh, M. T., & Salloum, I. M. (2020). Bimaristān Arghun al-Kamili in Aleppo, Syria: A Mental Hospital with Unique Architecture Designed to Meet Patient Need in Medieval Islam (1354 AD). *Arab Journal of Psychiatry*, *31*(2), 191–195.

Ak, A. Ş. (2017*). Avrupa ve Türk-İslâm Medeniyeti'nde müzikle tedavi tarihi, gelişimi ve uygulamaları*. Ötüken Yayınları.

Al-Gharbi, M. (2021). People of the book: Empire and social science in the Islamic commonwealth period. *Socius*, 7. https://doi.org/10.1177/23780231211021200

Al-Majūsī, 'Alī ibn al-'Abbās. (n.d.). *Kitab Kamil al-Sina'a = Al-Kitab al-Malaki* (Vol. 2). [al-Qahīrah] : Bulaq. (930–994). Retrieved May 30, 2023, from https://archive.org/details/b30095396_0002/page/n13/mode/2up

Ataseven, A. (1985). Tarihimizde Vakfedilmiş Sağlık Müesseseleri" Darü'ş-şifalar".

Awaad, R., & Ali, S. (2015). Obsessional disorders in al-balkhi's 9th-century treatise: Sustenance of the body and soul. *Journal of Affective Disorders*, *180*, 185–189. https://doi.org/10.1016/j.jad.2015.03.003

Awaad, R., & Ali, S. (2016). A modern conceptualization of phobia in al-Balkhi's 9th-century treatise: Sustenance of the Body and Soul. *Journal of Anxiety Disorders*, *37*, 89–93. doi:10.1016/j.janxdis.2015.11.003

Awaad, R., Mohammad, A., Elzamzamy, K., Fereydooni, S., & Gamar, M. (2019). *Mental Health in the Islamic Golden Era: The Historical Roots of Modern Psychiatry*. Islamophobia and Psychiatry.

Awaad, R., Conn, Y. S., Kolkailah, N., el-Haddad, H., Ali, S., & Fereydooni, S. (2022). From Alchemy to Psychiatry: A glimpse into the ethics and mental health practices of tenth-century Muslim physician Abū Bakr al-Rāzī. *Harvard Review of Psychiatry*, 30(5), 323–326. https://doi.org/10.1097/hrp.0000000000000347

Awaad, R., & Nursoy-Demir, M. (2023). Melodies in the hospital courtyard: A comparative history of Ottoman music therapy in the early modern period (c. 1400–1800). *The Arts in Psychotherapy*, *86*, 102092. https://doi.org/10.1016/j.aip.2023.102092

Badri, M. (2013). *Abu Zayd al-Balkhi's sustenance of the soul: The cognitive behavior therapy of a ninth century physician*. International Institute of Islamic Thought (IIIT).

Bahammam, Ahmed & Almeneessier, Aljohara & Pandi-Perumal, Seithikurippu R. (2018). Medieval Islamic scholarship and writings on sleep and dreams. *Annals of Thoracic Medicine*, 12. doi:10.4103/atm.ATM_162_17.

Canino, G., & Alegría, M. (2008). Psychiatric diagnosis - is it universal or relative to culture?. *Journal of Child Psychology and Psychiatry, and Allied Disciplines*, *49*(3), 237–250. https://doi.org/10.1111/j.1469-7610.2007.01854.x

Daher, A. M. (2015). I'maret Al Mujamaat oua Almabany Altibyah fi Al Islam (Al Bimaristānat). *Markaz Dirassat Al Imara Al Islamyah Al Alamy.* https://www.alukah.net/culture/0/91400/عمارة-المجمعات-والمباني-الطبية-البيمارستانات-في-الإسلام-PDF/

Dashti, R. (2020). Investigating the structure and organization of hospitals in Islamic Civilization: From the middle of the second century to the middle of the eighth century AH. *IJMEHM*, *13*, 75–90. https://doi.org/https://ijme.tums.ac.ir/article-1-6224-en.html

Deuraseh, N., & Abu Talib, M. (2005). Mental health in Islamic medical tradition. *The International Medical Journal*, *4*(2), 76–79.

Dols, M. W. (1992). *Majnūn: The Madman in medieval Islamic society*. Clarendon Press.

Erer, S., & Atıcı, E. (2010). *Selçuklu ve Osmanlılarda Müzikle Tedavi Yapılan Hastaneler. 36*(1), 29–32. https://dergipark.org.tr/en/pub/uutfd/issue/35281/391528

Evliya Çelebi. (2006). *Günümüz Türkçesiyle Evliya Çelebi Seyahatnamesi: Konya, Kayseri, Antakya, Şam, Urfa*, Maraş, *Sivas, Gazze, Sofya, Edirne, 3. Cilt-1. Kitap.* Yapı Kredi Yayınları.

Fierro, C. (2022). How did early North American clinical psychologists get their first personality test? Carl Gustav Jung, the Zurich School of Psychiatry, and the development of the "Word Association Test" (1898–1909). *History of Psychology*, *25*(4), 295–321. https://doi.org/10.1037/hop0000218

Gevrekzâde, H. (1794). *Neticetü'l-fikriyye fī Tedbir-i vilâdetü'l-bikriyye.*

Gorini, R. (2002). Attention and care to madness during the Islamic Middle Ages in Syria: The example of bimaristān al-Arghun from princely palace to bimaristān. *Journal of International Society for the History of Islamic Medicine*, *2*, 40–42.

Gorini, R. (2007). Bimaristāns and mental health in two different areas of the Medieval Islamic world. *Journal of International Society for the History of Islamic Medicine*, *6–7*, 16–20. https://www.ishim.net/ishimj/JISHIM11_12_13_14.pdf#page=22

Haque, A. (2004). Psychology from Islamic perspective: Contributions of early Muslim scholars and challenges to contemporary Muslim psychologists. *Journal of Religion and Health*, *43*(4), 357–377. https://doi.org/10.1007/s10943-004-4302-z

Hezel, D. M., & Simpson, H. B. (2019). Exposure and response prevention for Obsessive-compulsive disorder: A review and new directions. *Indian journal of psychiatry*, *61*(Suppl 1), S85–S92. https://doi.org/10.4103/psychiatry.IndianJPsychiatry_516_18

Hunke, S. (1997). *Le Soleil d'Allāh brille sur l'Occident*. Albin Michel

Ibn Abī Uṣaybiʿah, (2020). *ʿUyūn al-Anbāʾ fī Ṭabaqāt al-Aṭibbāʾ* [Best Accounts in the Classes of Physicians]. In Savage-Smith, E., Smith, S., & van Gelder G. J. (Trans.). *A Literary History of Medicine* (Vol. 134, *Ser. Handbook of Oriental Studies*. Section 1 *The Near and Middle East*). Brill. (Original work published 1245–1246 CE) https://doi.org/10.1163/37704_0668IbnAbiUsaibia.Tabaqatalatibba.lhom-tr-eng1

Issa, A. (1928). كتاب تاريخ البيمارستانات في الإسلام. ص87- كتاب تاريخ البيمارستانات في الإسلام- مارستان قلاوون [History of Bimaristāns in Islam]. https://shamela.ws/book/36083/85

Kahl, O. K. (2007). The Dispensatory of Ibn at-Tilmidh. *Islamic Philosophy, Theology and Science, 70.*

Kalender, R. (1987). Türk Musikisinde Kullanılan Makamların Tesirleri. *Ankara Üniversitesi İlahiyat Fakültesi Dergisi*, *29*(1–4), 361–376. https://dergipark.org.tr/en/download/article-file/2568940

Kirmayer, L. J., & Young, A. (1999). Culture and context in the evolutionary concept of mental disorder. *Journal of Abnormal Psychology*, *108*(3), 446–452. https://doi.org/10.1037/0021-843X.108.3.446

Lev, Y. (2005). *Charity, Endowments, and Charitable Institutions in Medieval Islam.* University Press of Florida. https://library.lol/main/56561F8BBEB3C3519E8E43DC738554B9

McDonald, G. (2014). Galen on mental illness: A physiological approach to Phrenitis. *Bulletin of the Institute of Classical Studies. 114*, 135–151. https://www.jstor.org/stable/44215141

Meyerhof, M. (1931). *Ali at-Tabari's "Paradise of Wisdom": One of the oldest Arabic compendiums of medicine* (Vol. 16). The University of Chicago Press on behalf of The History of Science Society.

Meyerhof, M. (1935). Thirty-three clinical observations by Rhazes (Circa 900 A.D.). *Isis*, *23*(2), 321–372. https://www.jstor.org/stable/224950

Miller, A. C. (2006). Jundi-Shapur, bimaristāns, and the rise of academic medical centres. *Journal of the Royal Society of Medicine*, *99*(12), 615–617.

Modanlou, H. D. (2008). A tribute to Zakariya Razi (865–925 AD), an Iranian pioneer scholar.

Murphey, R. (1992). Ottoman medicine and transculturalism from the sixteenth through the eighteenth century. *Bulletin of the History of Medicine*, *66*(3), 376–403.

Nagamia, H. F. (2003). Islamic medicine history and current practice. *JISHIM*, *2*, 19–30.

Nasr, S. H., & De Santillana, G. (1968). *Science and Civilization in Islam* (Vol. 16). Harvard University Press.

Nutton, V. (2006). Humoral theory. *Brill's New Pauly*. https://referenceworks.brillonline.com/entries/brill-s-new-pauly/humoral-theory-ct-e15208640?lang=de

Pérez, J., Baldessarini, R. J., Undurraga, J., & Sánchez-Moreno, J. (2012). Origins of psychiatric hospitalization in medieval Spain. *Psychiatric Quarterly*, *83*, 419–430.

Pitchon, V. (2016). Food and medicine in medieval Islamic hospitals : Preparation and care in accordance with dietetic principles. *Food and History*, *14*(1), 13–33. https://doi.org/10.1484/j.food.5.113853

Ragab, A. (2015). *The Medieval Islamic Hospital: Medicine, Religion, and Charity.* Cambridge University Press.

Saad, M., De Medeiros, R., & Mosini, A. C. (2017). Are we ready for a true biopsychosocial–spiritual model? The many meanings of "spiritual". *Medicines*, *4*(4), 79.

Saniotis A. (2012). Islamic medicine and evolutionary medicine: A comparative analysis. *The Journal of IMA*, *44*(1). https://doi.org/10.5915/44-1-8780

Sarı, N. (1982). *Halk Hekimliğinde ve Osmanlı Tıp Yazmalarında Akıl ve Sinir Hastalıklarının Tedavisi. 4.*

Sarı, N. (1986). *The Classification of Mental Diseases in the Ottoman Medical Manuscripts/Osmanlı Tıp Yazmalarında Akıl Hastalıklarının Sınıflandırılması.* https://www.academia.edu/47147221/The_Classification_of_Mental_Diseases_in_the_Ottoman_Medical_Manuscripts_Osmanl%C4%B1_T%C4%B1p_Yazmalar%C4%B1nda_Ak%C4%B1l_Hastal%C4%B1klar%C4%B1n%C4%B1n_S%C4%B1n%C4%B1fland%C4%B1r%C4%B1lmas%C4%B1

Sarı, N. (1988). *Cerrahiyetü'l-Haniye'de Dağlama Yoluyla Mâl-i Hülyâ Tedavisi ve Akupunktur Yöntemi İle Karşılaştırılması. 2.* https://www.academia.edu/47131640/Cerrahiyet%C3%BCl_Haniyede_Da%C4%9Flama_Yoluyla_M%C3%A2l_i_H%C3%BCly%C3%A2_Tedavisi_ve_Akupunktur_Y%C3%B6ntemi_%C4%B0le_Kar%C5%9F%C4%B1la%C5%9Ft%C4%B1r%C4%B1lmas%C4%B1

Sarı, N. (1995). *Osmanlı Darüşşifalarına Tayin Edilecek Görevlilerde Aranan Nitelikler.* https://www.academia.edu/47132902/Osmanl%C4%B1_Dar%C3%BC%C5%9F%C5%9Fifalar%C4%B1na_Tayin_Edilecek_G%C3%B6revlilerde_Aranan_Nitelikler

Sarı, N. (2016). *A Review of Ottoman Court Records on Mental Diseases.* https://www.academia.edu/45426699/A_Review_of_Ottoman_Court_Records_on_Mental_Diseases

Sarı, N. (2020, January 1). *Osmanlı Darüşşifasında Tedavi*. Afyon and Istanbul International Turkish-Islamic Medical History And Ethics Congresses (2018–2019) Proceedings Book, Konya. https://www.academia.edu/46571791/Osmanl%C4%B1_Dar%C3%BC%C5%9F%C5%9Fifas%C4%B1nda_Tedavi

Sarı, N., Tuğ, R., İzgöer, A. Z., & Okutan, M. Y. (2003). *Klasik Dönem İlaç Hazırlama Yöntemleri ve Terkipleri*. Novartis. https://www.academia.edu/49431918/Klasik_D%C3%B6nem_%C4%B0la%C3%A7_Haz%C4%B1rlama_Y%C3%B6ntemleri_ve_Terkipleri

Scalenghe, S. (2014). *Disability in the Ottoman Arab World, 1500–1800: Cambridge Studies in Islamic Civilization*. Cambridge University Press. https://doi.org/10.1017/CBO9781107045309

Shefer-Mossensohn, M. (2009). *Ottoman Medicine: Healing and Medical Institutions, 1500–1700*. State University of New York Press.

Shefer-Mossensohn, M. (2015). *Science among the Ottomans: The cultural creation and exchange of knowledge*. University of Texas Press.

Singer, P. N. (2018). Galen's pathological soul: Diagnosis and therapy in ethical and medical texts and contexts. In *Mental Illness in Ancient Medicine*. Brill. https://doi.org/10.1163/9789004362260_016

Syed, I. B. (1981). Islamic medicine: 1000 Years Ahead of its times. *Journal of the Islamic Medical Association of North America*, *13*(1). https://doi.org/10.5915/13-1-11925

Şengül, E. (2015). Edirne Sultan Bayezid II Hospital. *Turk Neurosurgery*, *25*(1), 8.

Şuuri, H. E. (1677). *Ta'dîlü'l-emzice fî hıfzi sıhhatü'l-beden (Adjustment of Temperaments in Protecting Health of the Body)*. National Library of Turkey (A.E.T.b, Box 66 & 68).

Ṭabarī, ʿAlī ibn Sahl Rabban. (n.d.). *Firdaws al-ḥikmah*. *Firdaws al-ḥikmah* فردوس الحكمة *Ṭabarī, ʿAlī ibn Sahl Rabban* طبري، علي بن سهل ربن. Retrieved June 13, 2023, from https://www.qdl.qa/archive/81055/vdc_100023062750.0x000001

Tabatabaei, S. M., & Jafari-Mehdiabad, A. (2020). Rhazes' pioneer viewpoints about psychiatry, neurology and neuroscience. *Journal of medical ethics and history of medicine*, *13*, 21. https://doi.org/10.18502/jmehm.v13i21.4863

Tavernier, J. B. (1684). A New Relation of the Inner-Part of the Grand Seignior's Seraglio. Moses Pitt at the Angel in St. Paul's Church-yard.

Tibi S. (2006). Al-Razi and Islamic medicine in the 9th century. *Journal of the Royal Society of Medicine*, *99*(4), 206–207. https://doi.org/10.1177/014107680609900425

Tudela, B. (1907). In M. N. Adler (Trans.). *The Itinerary of Benjamin of Tudela*. Phillip Feldheim, Inc. (Original work published c. 12th century).

Tunaboylu-İkiz, T. (1999). Türk psikiyatri tarihi ve psikanalizin yeri. *Psikoloji Çalışmaları*, *21*, 159–168.

Turabi, A. H. (2005). *Gevrekzâde Hâfız Hasan Efendi ve mûsikî risâlesi* [Gevrekzâde Hâfız Hasan Efendi and his music treatise]. Rağbet Yayınları.

Yassine, R. (2020). *The Role of Islamic Civilization in the Evolution and Development of Medical Thinking*. Doctoral dissertation, Sidi Mohamed Ben Abdellah University, Morocco. https://cdim.fmp-usmba.ac.ma/mediatheque/e_theses/157-20.pdf

Yüksel-Özkaya, Ş. (2016). Osmanlı'nın Tıp Anlayışını ve Akıl Hastalarına Yaklaşımını Belirleyen Faktörler İle Bu Anlayışın "Mâ-Hazar" da Tezâhürü. *Bildiriler Kitabı-II*, 305.

5 A Haven of Wellness

Unveiling the Healing Architecture of Maristāns

Manar Ghamian

Introduction

Whether entering a maristān in Damascus, Baghdad, Cairo, or Istanbul, the visitor had a large ornamented and welcoming doorway that not only opened to the courtyard but also opened and expanded the visitor's heart. Tweets of songbirds deluged guests who set foot into the building. The winding corridor with skylight openings ushered visitors away from the hustle and bustle of city life and into the serene and embracing courtyard. The central fountain and its cascading waters glimmered under the daylight from the open skies above while echoing nature's life-giving cooling rivers. Seating areas in the courtyard offered an unobstructed view of the celestial heavens that lifted the spirit and settled the body. Storytellers, musicians, and personal companions serenaded the courtyard with tales of heroes of the ancient past, litanies, and tunes that play at the strings of the heart. All the while, gentle winds cooled by the streaming water fountain in the courtyard refreshingly carried the scent of wall-climbing jasmine to the occupants of every hall, room, and corridor.

It would be forgiven if, upon reading the description above, one would imagine that this was the description of a royal Abbasid courtyard, a Mamlūk palace, or an Ottoman *Saray* (royal palace). Yet, it is a composite description of a maristān. Unlike 19th and 20th century hospitals, whose architecture was unquestionably shaped by Louis Sullivan's famous proclamation that form follows function, the architecture of maristāns was more than just functional (Sullivan, 1896).

One such way that maristāns' architecture transcended functionality was that their architectural design observably found commonality with other important public institutions in the traditional Muslim city, such as the mosque, the *madrasah*, and bazaars. Underpinned by the principle of *Tawhîd* (Unity and Oneness), these institutions were inspired by a singular source that brushed upon them a commonality not of design and building material but of shared sacredness, experience, and ethos. The renowned contemporary architect Juhani Pallasmaa noted that 'when you enter a building, the building enters you too' (Debartolo, 2019). Buildings are not merely spaces that people

DOI: 10.4324/9781003329589-5

occupy but are objects that evoke an inner response within their occupants. Pallasmaa argues that it is through the engaging of all senses—physical and spiritual—that the body and soul become the focal point of experience within architectural buildings (Pallasmaa, 2005). Put another way, architecture that is life-enhancing holistically engages all senses. The architecture of maristāns was not merely functional; it also complemented its built purpose by engaging its occupants' senses: physical, psychological, and spiritual.

Environmental Setting, Sensory Stimulation, and Well-being in ibn Bi'albak's Writings

The effect of the environmental setting on well-being did not escape physicians and those involved in establishing maristāns in mediaeval Islāmic civilisations. One such example is the physician ibn Bi'albak (d.1277) of the 13th century CE. In his book, *The Delighter of the Soul*, ibn Bi'albak discusses various stimulants that delight the soul (Ibn Qadi Bi'albak, 2006). It is worth noting that ibn Bi'albak is not restricting his work to that which brings pleasure to the body but rather that which brings joy to the soul. The soul refers to the unified sense of self, which includes the body, mind, and soul. He notes that the soul's experiences of joy and happiness are more conducive to swift healing and the regaining of strength following an illness. Ibn Bi'albak's understanding of the psycho-somatic relationship was not novel within the Muslim medical tradition, as it closely aligned with even earlier Muslim physicians such as Abu Zayd al-Balkhī (d. 934) of the 9th century (Deuraseh & Abu Talib, 2005). As such, ibn Bi'albak included various sources of joy that have an overall positive and healthy effect on the whole self.

In the chapter addressing how sight brings joy to the soul, ibn Bi'albak first established his framework of what sight is capable of perceiving (Ibn Bi'albak, 2006). He noted that sight is not limited to colours and shapes. Rather, sight is essential in perceiving twenty-six other qualities: light, darkness, edges, size, distance, proximity, position, form, connectedness, disconnectedness, count, movement, stillness, smoothness, ruggedness, density, translucency, shadow, beauty, ugliness, brightness, contrast, laughter, sadness, viscosity, and dryness. He further noted, 'know that the soul finds joy and pleasure in looking towards spacious areas...such as gardens that contain a variety of beautiful colours'. He also observed that public baths of his time often contained 'images drawn with dyes that bring strength to the body and spirit' (Ibn Bi'albak, 2006, p. 60). Similarly, ibn Bi'albak dedicated chapters on scents, sounds, and tastes and their positive role in bringing harmony, balance, strength, and happiness to the soul. Essentially, ibn Bi'albak asserted the importance of what is referred to today as fully embodied experiences in healing and recovery.

Ibn Bi'albak's writings are of great significance for the topic of maristān architecture for two reasons. First, ibn Bi'albak had worked as a physician in several Levante-area maristāns, including the prominent Nūr al-Dīn Maristān of Damascus, where King Muthafar placed him as the head of physicians, oculists, and surgeons (Ibn Abī Uṣaybiʿah, 1882). Second, and more importantly, during his capacity as chief of physicians and director of the maristān, ibn Bi'albak oversaw the expansion of the Damascene maristān by buying the adjacent land and 'expanding its halls and building it up exquisitely so that cascading waters ran through it, making it complete and perfect' (Ibn Abī Uṣaybiʿah, 1882). As such, it is fair to assume that ibn Bi'albak's attitudes regarding the potential of the physical environment and its impact on patients' psychological and physical well-being guided the expansion project and shaped the maristān's design. In his conclusion, ibn Bi'albak commended the merits of cultivating spaces that positively engage as many of the five senses as possible and, as such, allowed for multiple avenues for delight to reach the soul and, in turn, improve overall physical well-being (Ibn Bi'albak, 2006).

Unfortunately, there is no surviving conclusive evidence, by way of architectural blueprints or manuscripts, that uncovers the underlying intent of maristāns' architectural designs. However, examining the writings of physicians who were involved in the building of maristāns, such as ibn Bi'albak, has shed a clarifying light on this issue. Examining their writings regarding the impact of the physical environment on well-being against common design features of maristāns strongly suggests that maristāns were built with more than just function in mind. Rather, they met the functional needs of hospitals *and* complemented healing through sensorial engagement and careful architectural designs that, through form and symbol, offered conditions conducive to healing the body, mind, and spirit. A quick and straightforward surveying of surviving maristāns leaves little doubt that they were also built with beauty, craftsmanship, and human dignity in mind.

Hospital Design in Modern Discourse

Shifting, momentarily, to contemporary discourses on hospital architecture reveals the growing empirical evidence of the relationship between physical settings and their effect on both psychological and physical well-being (Rubin, 1998; Ulrich et al., 2004; Ulrich et al., 2008). For example, Ulrich's simple yet seminal study revealed that patients in rooms with a window overlooking a garden have demonstrably shorter recovery times post-operatively compared to patients in rooms with a window overlooking a brick wall (Ulrich, 1984). In his article titled Healing by Design, Horsburgh identified four qualities of hospital design that positively contribute to patients' well-being—orientation, connection, scale, and symbolism (Horsburgh, 1995).

The qualities that Horsburgh identified addressed the relationship between people and their physical environment. Orientation concerns the occupant's ability to locate themselves within their immediate and larger physical environment adequately. Connection is a quality that offers a patient the sense of being appropriately connected to both their social and physical environments while offering privacy from both when needed. Architectural scale refers to building proportions in relation to its occupants. The scale that contributes to patients' well-being, Horsburgh noted, is one that is neither too grand that would make the occupant feel little and insignificant nor should it be too small that it would be experienced as cramped and uncomfortable. Lastly, Horsburgh argued that well-designed hospital buildings promote health and well-being by conveying symbolic meanings of security, safety, and sanitation (Horsburgh, 1995).

What follows is an examination of how the architectural design of maristāns contributed to its occupants' physical, psychological, and spiritual well-being through Horsburgh's fourth quality of hospital architecture: symbolism. The qualities of orientation, connection, and scale will also be examined where applicable. Understanding the symbolic meanings of maristān architecture will build on two pillars: an Islāmic cosmological framework and the historical origins of maristāns concerning the traditional Muslim city and its architecture.

Symbolism, Islāmic Cosmology, and Maristān Architecture

Put simply, symbols are often, though not exclusively, material objects that represent abstract or intangible concepts. This is built upon the premise that symbols can embody abstract concepts beyond the limits of their materiality (Speaks, 2021). In relation to Islāmic architecture, design features act as material symbols that reference concepts from the 'ālam al-ġhayb (unseen and immaterial world; *The Qur'ān*, 13:9, 16:77, 6:59, 3:44). Here, we must refer to the field of cosmology; a field of study concerned with the origins, form, and nature of the universe.

According to Islāmic cosmology, the structure of reality consists of three levels of existence (Umar, 2002). The material world, *dunyā*' (literally, the 'lowest'), is the lowest level of existence. Above it is the *'ālam al-ġhayb* (unseen or immaterial world), which is intricately tied to the lower material world. The material world of form and matter (also known as 'ālam *al-shahadah,* or the witnessable world) is an embodiment of *ma'ānī* (meanings) found in the immaterial world (Ikhwān al-Ṣafā', 1984; Umar, 2002). As the 20th-century Sufi scholar Muḥammad ibn al-Habīb (d. 1972) notes in his poetry, 'The cosmos is truly [the] only spirit [meaning] existing in forms' (Al-Habib, 2017, p. 208). Above the immaterial world in the levels of existence is The Divine Reality. The immaterial world, and thus, by extension, the material world, is understood to be manifestations of God's names and creative attributes.[1] Written metaphorically, the material world is a shadow resulting from casting Divine Light onto the immaterial world (Figure 5.1).

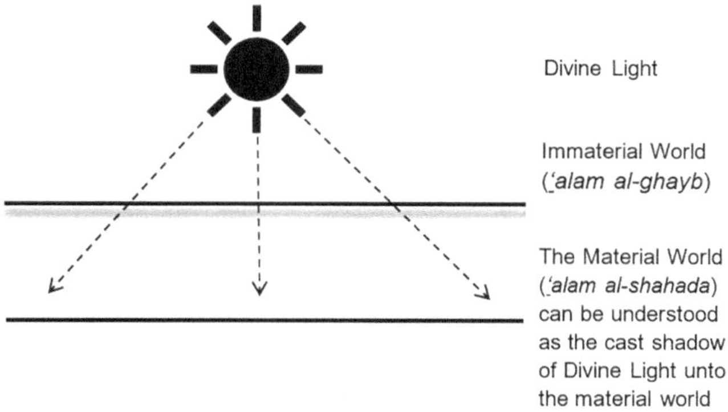

Figure 5.1 Levels of existence according to Islāmic cosmology.

As such, symbolism can be understood as the representation of one level of reality by referencing a corresponding reality on a different level (Coomaraswamy, 1980). As Akkach (2005) notes, 'symbols of the sacred reveal something of the sacred itself and produce an experience of sacredness in those who are experiencing [the symbols]' (p. 12). It is this capacity of symbolism in Islāmic architecture, that is, to produce an experience of sacredness that permitted maristāns to provide healing not only within its walls but also by and through them.

An investigation of symbolism in the Qur'ān further sheds light on the role of symbolism in architectural design. The Qur'ān repeatedly presses its readers to reflect on the many *āyāt* (signs and symbols) in the created world as a means to ascertain higher realities of the unseen world (*The Qur'ān*, 41:53). God Himself tells us to reflect on His creation (*The Qur'ān*, 3: 191), not Himself, as no human reflection can truly grasp His essence (*The Qur'ān*, 6:103). As such, the path to witnessing God in this life is through reflecting upon symbols in His creation. Symbols, the Qur'ān affirms, are detailed and made clear so that humanity may have a pathway to reorient themselves back to God (2:266, 7:174). This concept of returning back to God is called *tawbah*.

The turning to God is synonymous with a return to the uncorrupted primordial nature, or *fiṭrah* (*The Qur'ān*, 30:30). *Fiṭrah* originates in the spirit of humans before their earthly existence. However, in relation to the world it exists in, *fiṭrah* can be understood as one's alignment with the realities of the seen and unseen worlds (Mohamed, 1996). Furthermore, because it is part of human nature to occupy oneself with the lowly world (*The Qur'ān*, 7:146, 10:7), humans are always in need of being reminded of greater and unseen realities (*The Qur'ān*, 30:7). Islāmic architecture, with symbols that speak directly to the soul and not the intellect, brings humans to a state of harmony within themselves, the world around them, and Divine Reality.

This is the almost palpable feeling of expansion, providence, and safety that is experienced upon entering traditionally built structures that were part of historical Muslim civilisations.

Furthermore, the potency of sacred symbols is independent of the pre-existing knowledge of the connection between the symbol and what it represents (Akkach, 2005). The meaning contained within such sacred symbols is not constructed but rather revealed and experienced. The meaning of an object or symbol transcends its physical boundaries. Its meaning is found in what it points to by way of some experience. In other words, meaning is relational, and the meaning of an object would be the possible experiences it affords us—either now, in the past, or in the future (Johnson, 2015).

With this understanding of symbolism and what it may afford to those who experience its meanings, we will briefly explore the various design features of maristāns, their symbolic meanings, and their contribution to healing.

Maristāns and the Architecture of Muslim Cities

To speak of the maristān and its architectural design, one must see maristāns as one of the many institutions that complementarily attended to the physical, psychological, and spiritual well-being of residents. The first of these institutions is the mosque, located at the heart of the traditional city. The mosque acts as the city's spiritual centre and sets the tone for the city's character. Just like the sound of the call of prayer that emanates from the mosque to the rest of the city, the mosque also radiates its spiritual and architectural identity to the city's civil structures and institutions: homes, bazaars, *madāris*, and the maristān. The *madrasah*, often established within a mosque complex, was developed to serve as a fully integrated educational institution that taught religious sciences, philosophy, mathematics, and medicine (Makdisi, 1984). Relevant to both the mosque and *madrasah*, Sufi *zāwiyāt* (lodges) were dedicated spaces that tended to the needs of the Sufi path and its followers. These *zāwiyāt* functioned as a space for prayer, spiritual formation, and character refinement.

While the mosque, *madrasah*, maristān, and *zāwiyāt* were separate establishments, each serving a unique purpose and need, they shared a unified underlying architectural identity within the traditional city. As the contemporary, traditional architect 'Abdel-Wahīd al-Wakīl (1984) noted, the Islāmic city had a tangible identity that depended not on the uniformity of design or materials but on the unity of traditional principles that are found in the revealed Word, the Qur'ān. That is why the maristān, while uniquely designed and built, seamlessly fits within the Muslim city and its surroundings.

While the architecture of maristāns was developing in the 8th and 9th centuries, Islāmic architecture started with the building of the Prophetic Mosque in Medina shortly after the *Hijrah* (The Prophet Muḥammad's [ﷺ] migration from Mecca to Medina in 622 CE). All Islāmic arts, including architecture, find their roots and origins in the ornamentation of the Divine Word, the Qur'ān (Nasr, 1987). The development of Islāmic architecture was chiefly concerned with constructing and ornamenting the primary space of Qur'ānic recitation, the mosque. Later, Islāmic architecture branched out to include other civilian structures, leaving its mark on schools, palaces, bazaars, and maristāns. It becomes clear that Islāmic architecture was not just about stylistic choices or the usage of specific shapes, symbols, or colour palettes. Rather, Islāmic architecture, having grown from the mosque's design, imbues the mundane with the sacredness of the revealed word and its pearls of wisdom; it aims to put into form the inner teachings of the Qur'ān. The concern with magnifying, ornamenting, and centring the Qur'ān, and by extension its symbols, in the lives of Muslims is precisely what puts the 'Islāmic' in Islāmic art and architecture.

Traditional Muslim artists, including architects, are guided in their artwork by Qur'ānic teachings. Their art form becomes a manifestation of the realities and meanings of the Qur'ānic revelation as they take root in the artist's heart (Nasr, 2010). As an example, the geometrical designs and motifs, common in various forms of Islāmic art, in their repetition and illusion of infinity, aim to not only reflect God's Infinite Treasures (*khazāin al-ġhayb*) but also to nourishingly draw from them as they represent the unseen in the material world. The symmetry and intricate patterns of these designs represent Divine Order in creation, allowing those who encounter the art an opportunity to experience God's Creative Wisdom despite the apparent chaos of the human experience.

Although bazaars, maristāns, and palaces were not built with overt spiritual significance, the relationship between the art, the artist, and the inner meanings of the Qur'ān denotes that the esoteric realities of Qur'ānic revelation architecturally infused these institutions. Hence, Islāmic architecture gives all its buildings a unified architectural character and identity. At the core of Islāmic revelation is the concept of *Tawhîd*, the assertion of the Unity of Allāh (ﷻ) that there is only one God. The concept of *Tawhîd* is at the centre of every Islāmic science and art form (Nasr, 1987). In Islāmic architecture, *Tawhîd* as a concept is multivalent. In the mosque, *Tawhîd* can be witnessed when worshippers in the congregation pray as one in unison. On an individual level, *Tawhîd* is about witnessing the Oneness of God. Through the framework of maristān architecture, *Tawhîd* can be understood as 'to make into one' or 'to make whole'. Thus, through its design and symbolic meanings, *Tawhîd*, specifically as it is embodied in the architecture of maristāns, can contribute by bringing its patients and visitors to a state of wholeness, equilibrium, and balance.

Upon its arrival unto this earth, the soul was separated from the Divine Reality and lost sight of God's Oneness. Thus, the human journey on this earth is the striving to reclaim the state of *fiṭrah* that affirms and witnesses God's Oneness (*Tawhîd*) in word and action. Islāmic art, including architecture, embodies the Qur'ānic realities of *Tawhîd* and symbolically conveys its meanings, constantly reminding humans of their *fiṭrah*. Through symbolism, maristān architecture reinforces this state of wholeness, balance, and harmony in its occupants.

Healing, Fiṭrah, and Design Features

Building maristāns as part of a larger complex comprised of a mosque, *madrasah*, mausoleum, and other buildings was common. As indicated above, the architecture of the maristān aimed to bring patients to their state of *fiṭrah*. To do so, the architect abstracted principles of Divine Architecture as observed around them in nature and integrated them into the architectural design of the maristān (Nasr, 1987). In a sense, traditionally designed maristāns embodied in their very structure the healing properties of nature within the building. The traditional aspiration to reproduce the healing effects of nature on the occupants of a building is today captured under the contemporary term biophilic design (Gillis & Gatersleben, 2015). As more research and empirical evidence on the impact of nature on health and well-being becomes available, the integration of nature in architectural design is eagerly anticipated.

As for the traditional Muslim architects of the past, nature was not only a source of artistic inspiration but also a source of healing. The Qur᾿ān states that just as God created humans upon a primordial nature, the natural order is also created upon a primordial state (6:14,79, 12:101, 14:10, 35:1, 39:46, 42:11). Being of the greatest natural order, the primordial states of humans and nature are in essence one; both issuing from the One. In its uncorrupted primordial state, encounters with nature press upon humans and remind them of their own innate *fiṭrah*. The Qur᾿ān's injunctions to traverse the earth and contemplate its symbols as a pathway to returning to *fiṭrah* highlight nature's capacity to bring humans to a state of balance. This remembering of the *fiṭrah* is experienced as becoming whole, complete, and in harmony with oneself.

By accepting the traditional view of nature's capacity to remind humans of their true nature and thus return them to a state of balance, it should come as no surprise that the use of natural sounds, light, scent, and earthly materials for therapeutic practices within maristāns was well-documented (Ergin, 2015). Seldom discussed, however, is the impact that the architectural design of the maristān had on its occupants with regard to their healing and recovery. The meaning represented in an architectural form is experientially intuited by the visitor. This meaning leaves its imprint on the soul. If it is a positive meaning, as it would be in a maristān, it moves the patients along in their healing process by bringing them closer to their *fiṭrah* and, hence, a state of balance.

Entrance

The entrance of the maristān presents the first architectural feature that the visitors would experience as they walk through its doors. Similar to a mosque's entrance, the entrance of a maristān marks the transition between the exterior and the interior, from the less holy street to the more sacred place of healing. The entrance to the maristān had two common features that expressed invitation and safety. First, the portal extended to the full height of the façade of the building, expressing that the doorway to God's grace and healing is open and always accessible (Gabr, 1992). The large inviting portal would have evoked hope for healing as it echoed a prophetic Ḥadīth stating that for every illness God created, He also created a cure (Al-Bukhârî, 5678). Second, the recessed portal drew the gaze inward, emphasising invitation and creating a sense of safety and protection while transitioning the visitor to a more sacred space (Ragab, 2015). The recessed arch evoked the imagery and symbolic meaning of the Qur'ānic Cave, which was a source of protection and safety for the young men fleeing persecution (*The Qur'ān*, 18) (Figure 5.2).

In addition, the entrance was often in the shape of an arch, with a quadrangular base and a curved top. In sacred geometry, the square shape corresponds to the terrestrial realm, and the curved top represents the celestial world (Badawi, 2021). Thus, the arch, in its vertical orientation, represents a transcendence from the terrestrial world to the celestial heavens. The arch's pointed top symbolises the journey of the ascension of the soul from the world to the heavens (Gabr, 1992). Thus, the symbolism of the maristān arch affirms the human experience's multidimensional facets (physical and spiritual) and, by extension, the interconnectivity of the soul and body in relation to well-being and health.

On the psychological level, the entrance of the maristān undertakes the delicate issue of negotiating an architectural scale that affords the building the space required to fulfil the whole range of hospital duties yet remains congruous with a space of healing, safety, and warmth that places the human experience at the centre above all. Figure 5.1 depicts how the Qalāwūn Maristān portal extends the full façade of the building, yet it does not do so at the expense of making the visitor feel minuscule or insignificant. This is achieved by creating within the large-sized portal a smaller human-scale doorway that does not overwhelm the visitors upon entry but embraces them into the security and protection of the maristān. A similar observation can be made of the Bīmaristān Arghun al-Kamili portal in Figure 5.2.

The Corridor

Upon entering the doorway, the visitor does not suddenly find themselves in the main hall of the maristān or a courtyard. Similar to modern hospitals that gradually transition to their desired unit, the visitor to the maristān is tasked with walking through a series of small halls followed by small corridors (such as in Nūr al-Dīn Maristān in Damascus) or an often-long corridor with multiple bends (as is the case in the Qalāwūn Maristān) before

Figure 5.2 Street entrance of Qalāwūn Maristān in Cairo. The height of the doorway and the recessed design is common with other maristāns.

reaching the main courtyard. The corridor and its bends may have served a utilitarian function by helping align the maristān with the street or the *qiblah* (the direction to Kaaba, Mecca). Esoterically, the long and bending corridor invites the visitor to detach and detoxify from the *dunyāh*, which is often the cause of many psychological and physiological ailments (Gabr, 1992). The twists and turns of the corridor or the successive small halls create a

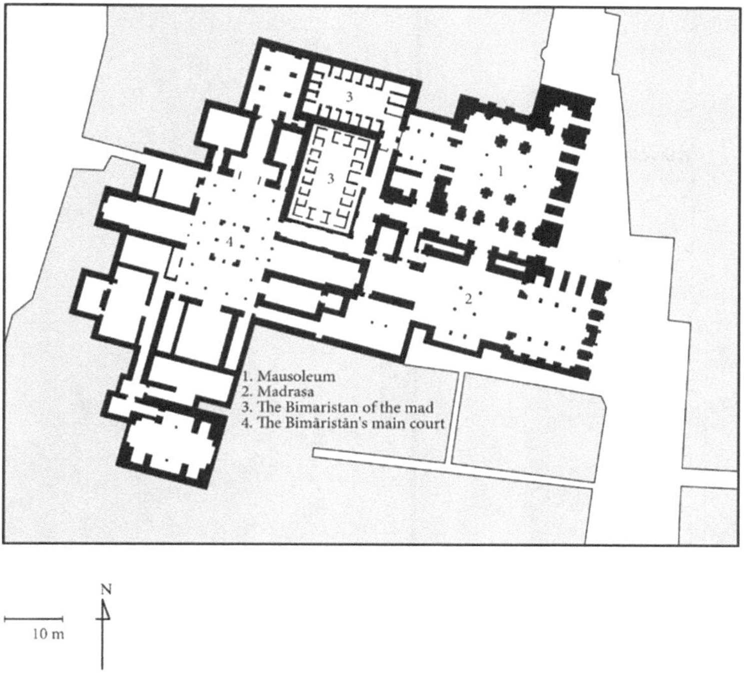

Figure 5.3 Plan of Qalāwūn Maristān in Cairo showcasing the entrance to the maristān through a long and bending corridor.

physical, and more importantly a psychological, distance between the visitor and the troubles of the outer world. The 'shedding' of the *dunyāh* with every turn of the corridor is in line with the Sufi concept of *taẖhliyah* (purification). Following *taẖhliyah*, the visitor is made ready for the *taḥliyah* (adornment) offered in the maristān as they enter the calm, serene, and expansive courtyard (Figure 5.3).

The Courtyard

The courtyard was a ubiquitous feature found in maristāns across the Muslim world. It served both functional and symbolic purposes for the maristān and its users. Functionally, the courtyard provided a social space for communal outdoor activities and fresh air. When the courtyard was not filled with the recitation of the Qur'ān or the playing of *maqām music*, songbirds filled it with concerts against the soothing backdrop of water flowing from the fountain (McClary, 2021) (Figure 5.4).

Figure 5.4 Depiction of Qalāwūn Maristān courtyard showing musical instruments and the water fountain (Museum, n.d.).

The courtyard also provided maristān residents and visitors with a private viewing of the heavens. The heavens represent the vertical axis of spiritual orientation. God's Throne resides above the heavens, and the Qur᾽ān notes that the heavens are the direction from whence grace and provision descend to the earth (*The Qur᾽ān*, 51:22). For the patient, reflecting upon the heavenly canopy likely provided a calming stillness and a spiritual orientation that inspired introspection and contemplation (*The Qur᾽ān*, 16:16).

Considering Horsburgh's architectural qualities, the courtyard, in its centrality within the maristān, offered its occupants an anchoring space that kept them oriented to a unified centre, making wayfinding from private to common areas much easier. Furthermore, the courtyard played the starring role in giving maristān occupants a strong sense of connection, which is another key architectural quality as identified by Horsburgh. The courtyard bridged the occupant from the private quarters of the maristān into an open communal space that offered a connection to the natural world through the experience of light, water, sound, and the heavens above. Providing an outdoor space for patients who might be bound to the maristān for prolonged periods of time made the courtyard a predominantly necessary design feature.

Whereas the winding corridors leading into the courtyard intended to disconnect the maristān occupants from their worldly concerns, the courtyard maintained a necessary and healthy connection to society. The daily calls for prayers, public declarations of official mandates, and local announcements remain audible from within the courtyard. In relation to other maristān occupants, the courtyard simultaneously connected, potentially, all patients of the maristān and, with its many edges, walkways, and corners, created a space of differentiation for patients wishing to maintain personal space within a communal setting. The impact of courtyards in maristāns on their occupants can be further imagined, thanks to contemporary research on the role of open spaces in hospitals today. Using data from several mental health wards, McIntosh et al. (2022) noted that courtyards can offer a sense of connectedness, hope and optimism, identity, empowerment, meaning and purpose and safety and security.

The Water Fountain

Equally conspicuous in nearly all maristāns across the Muslim world, a water fountain typically adorned the courtyard's centre. It has been well-established that the water fountain was not used for ablution purposes in mediaeval Islāmic architecture, as ablution facilities were present elsewhere in all maristāns (Gabr, 1992). Water in the Islāmic tradition has multiple symbolic meanings. It represents the Throne of God (*The Qur'ān*, 11:7), the heavenly gardens (4:122), and the Sharia, which 'literally means a path leading to a watering place' (Coulson & El Shamsy, 2024). The Qur'ān uses the same word, *nazzala* (to bring down), about Qur'ānic revelation as well as life-giving rain. God, thus, draws parallels between the rain that brings life to the barren land and the *Qur'ān*, which blooms life into hearts that have hardened (*The Qur'ān,* 10:57). Both the Qur'ān and water, in the form of rain, are referenced in the Qur'ān as mercy. Thus, the water fountain symbolises the maristān's aspirations to be a spring of mercy and life to both the physical and spiritual realities (Figure 5.5).

As mentioned earlier, the water fountain in the courtyard symbolises God's Throne, as the water reflects the heavens, and God's Throne 'was above water' (*The Qur'ān*, 11:7). Attesting to that, in Nūr al-Dīn Maristān of Damascus, the water fountain's exterior is shaped as a square, which once again symbolises the terrestrial and material realm (see Figure 5.5). Meanwhile, the interior of the water fountain is octagonal in shape. The eight-sided interior symbolises God's Throne as the Qur'ān notes that the Throne is upheld by eight angels (69:17). Evoking through symbolism, the Throne of God and the grace that descends from it evokes God's Providence upon the courtyard, the maristān, and its patients. The symbolism of God's Throne in the maristān's courtyard further asserts God's Hand in the healing process (*The Qur'ān*, 26:80). In addition, the Qur'ān states, 'And We…made from water every living thing' (21:30). Centring the water fountain shifts the maristān from being a place for the ill to being a place for physical and spiritual healing and prosperity.

Figure 5.5 The water fountain of the Nūr al-Dīn Maristān in Damascus. The square-shaped exterior symbolises the terrestrial world, and the interior symbolises the throne of God carried by eight angels. Credit: Nasser Rabbat, courtesy of Aga Khan Documentation Center, MIT Libraries (AKDC@MIT).

Thanks to empirical research, it is clear that the benefits of water fountains in places of healing transcend (theists may insist that 'overflow' would be a more appropriate verb) from the spiritual into the physical and psychological. For example, Alvarsson et al. (2010) demonstrate that exposure to natural landscapes and sounds, including water flow, leads to quicker recovery following physiological and psychological stressors. Incorrectly thought to be of mere functional or aesthetic value, it is clear now that the water fountain perfectly encapsulates the intentionality behind maristān architecture and its splendour. Symbolically significant, sensorially enriching, aesthetically pleasing, and spatially and socially constructive, our understanding of the therapeutic benefits of water fountains continues to rise.

The Crestings

The view of the heavens offered by the maristān's courtyard was one that was interlocked with the building's crestings. In Islāmic architecture, crestings do not merely serve an aesthetic purpose; they also symbolise the interwoven nature of the physical and spiritual worlds (Gabr, 1992). The solid portion of the cresting represents the physical and material world, whereas the negative empty spaces represent the unseen world. A replica of negative space separates the solid parts. Typically, the solid portion starts with a broad base and

Figure 5.6 Building crestings in Islāmic architecture symbolise the constant interplay between the spiritual and physical worlds.

ends with a narrow tip. The gradual upward narrowing of the material represents the spiritual journey of ascension transcending the material world into the immaterial world. As for the negative space, it is the largest and widest at its top and then narrows as it reaches its base. Symbolically, this represents Divine Grace that descends from the heavens and makes its way to the terrestrial realm. Collectively, the solid and empty spaces symbolise the intimate relationship between the material body and the immaterial soul. In the context of the maristān, the relationship between body and soul, their interdependence, and the effects of each on the other cannot be overstated. This simple yet intentional design feature further impresses upon the maristān occupants the importance of their spiritual health in their search for physical healing (Figure 5.6).

Inscriptions

Common to all traditional Islāmic buildings, Qur'ānic inscriptions adorn the walls and imbue the structure with Divine Grace and blessings. In Nūr al-Dīn Maristān, the walls of one of the *iwāns* (halls) are adorned with three passages from the Qur'ān, all related to health, healing, and cure (Al-Tabba, 1982).[2] These verses not only establish the indisputable connection between the Islāmic tradition and maristāns but also affirm that healing is ultimately from and by God (*The Qur'ān*, 26:80). The visitor, thus, is reminded that while outwardly they seek healing from the hands of physicians, esoterically they must turn themselves to God, the ultimate source of healing.

Conclusion

While maristān architects from the mediaeval era did not subscribe to an epistemological framework that centres empirical evidence as the basis for design, upon review of the various design features, it is undoubtedly evident that maristāns were designed with keen intentionality. A quick survey of the most well-known maristāns demonstrates that certain design features spanned geographical boundaries and historical eras (see Table 5.1). The prevalence of these features, despite different eras, political rules, and cultures, strongly suggests deliberation and intentionality. As previously noted, each of these design features contributed to the psychological, spiritual, and ultimately physical well-being of maristān occupants. Through its sensorially engaging and symbolically loaded design features, maristān architecture cultivated an embodied and holistic experience within its patients.

Tawhîd underpinned the architectural identity of maristāns, tying it inseparably to a larger set of institutions that collectively attended to the holistic well-being of men and women (Keshavarzi & Ali, 2019). With *Tawhîd* at the foundation of its architecture, the ultimate aim of maristān architecture was to impart *Tawhîd*, understood as becoming whole, unto its occupants. Thus, engaging all of a patient's senses and faculties was imperative to attaining full physical and psychological well-being.

From within this framework, it is inconceivable for modern hospitals to attend to the needs of their patients while neglecting or perhaps even failing to acknowledge the spiritual dimensions of their patients' experiences. Biophilic design, which finds its inspiration in nature, can help create common sacred spaces of healing that transcend religious demarcations or architectural styles. As explained earlier, nature enjoys its lofty standing within healing because encounters with nature reinforce and remind humans of their primordial nature, which is an acknowledgement of the spirit and an invitation to its fulfilment. This is experienced through a sense of being whole and complete. Physiologically, this is measured through lower stress levels, improved mood, and quicker recovery, among other benefits (Thoma et al., 2018). As such, incorporating elements of nature within spaces of healing is firmly within the tradition that maristāns have advanced in centuries past. Designing spaces of healing with nature as a vital part of the design is low-lying fruit with immeasurable benefits.

Juhani Pallasmaa (2012) remarked, 'The door handle is the handshake of the building' (p. 62). If propping open the door handle is akin to shaking hands with a hospital, what, then, would entering into its halls, roaming its corridors, resting in its chairs, and laying in its rooms feel like? Would the all-encompassing embrace or clinch of space not have a considerable impact on the journey of healing? The space of healing cannot be thought of as secondary to the treatment, but it is an instrumental element on the path to recovery. As the architectural historian Hamlin (1940) remarked, 'The quality of the surroundings of the sick person may be as important in the cure as the specific therapeutic measures themselves' (p.712). It is time to recover the legacy of maristān architecture and bring holistic healing not only to spaces of healing but also through the spaces themselves.

Table 5.1 Common Design Features in Maristāns

Maristān Name	*Location*	*Large Entrance*	*Majaz/ or Corridor*	*Courtyard*	*Water Fountain*	*Inscriptions*	*Crestings/ Stalactites*
Bīmaristān Arghun al-Kamili	Aleppo	Yes	Yes	Yes	Yes	Yes	Yes
Al-Mansuri	Cairo	Yes	Yes	Yes	Yes	Yes	Yes
Nūr al-Dīn	Damascus	Yes	No	Yes	Yes	Yes	Yes
Edirne Sultan Bayazid II	Edirne	Yes	Yes	Yes	Yes	Yes	No
Divriği Ulu Camii ve Darüşşifası	Divrigi, Turkey	Yes	Yes	Yes	Yes	Yes	Yes
Granada Maristān	Granada	Yes	No	Yes	Yes	Yes	Unknown

Notes

1 Ikhwān al-Ṣafā (1984) note, in an address to the king of their time, 'Then know, O just king, that these forms, shapes, structures, and attributes, which you see in the world of bodies and material substances, are symbols, similitudes, and colours of those forms that are in the world of spirits, save that the latter are luminous and subtle, while the former is dark and dense. The relationship of the former to the latter is as the relationship between the paintings on the surfaces of boards and walls to the actual forms and shapes of the animals with flesh, blood, bones, and skin. Those forms in the spiritual world are the movers, while these are the moved. As for the ones below, they are motionless, speechless, sensible, decayable, corruptible, and perishable, while those [above] are rational, intelligible, spiritual, invisible, and durable'.

2 The first inscription is 'O mankind, there has come to you instruction from your Lord and healing for what is in the breasts and guidance and mercy for the believers' (*The Qur'ān*, 10:57).

The second inscription cites the words of Abraham as he said 'and when I am ill, it is He Who cures me' (*The Qur'ān*, 26:80).

The third inscription is 'Then eat from all the fruits and follow the ways of your Lord laid down [for you]. There emerges from their bellies a drink, varying in colours, in which there is healing for people. Indeed in that is a sign for a people who give thought' (*The Qur'ān*, 16:69).

References

Akkach, S. (2005). *Cosmology and Architecture in Premodern Islam: An Architectural Reading of Mystical Ideas*. State University of New York Press.

Al-Bukhârî, M. (n.d.). *There is no disease except its treatment.* sunnah.com - sayings and teachings of Prophet Muḥammad (ﷺ). https://sunnah.com/bukhari:5678

Al-Habib, M. I. (2017). In M. M. Al-Boumas-houli (Ed.), *The Diwan: Of Shaykh Muḥammad ibn al-Habib* (pp. 206–209). Diwan Press.

Al-Wakil, A.-W. (1984). Identity, tradition and architecture. In *Arab Architecture: Past and Present*. Arab British Chamber of Commerce.

Al-Tabba, Y. A. (1982). *The Architectural Patronage of Nur Al-Din, (*1146–1174*)* (Vols. I and II) ProQuest Dissertations Publishing. https://search.proquest.com/docview/303071490?pq-origsite=primo

Alvarsson, J. J., Wiens, S., & Nilsson, M. E. (2010). Stress recovery during exposure to nature sound and environmental noise. *International Journal of Environmental Research and Public Health*, *7*(3), 1036–1046. https://doi.org/10.3390/ijerph7031036

Badawi, M. (2021). *Spiritual Significance in Islāmic Architecture*. IV Publishing.

Coomaraswamy, A. K. (1980). Symbols. *Studies in Comparative Religion*, *14*, 1.

Coulson, N. J., & El Shamsy, A. (2024, January 3). Sharia. *Encyclopedia Britannica*. https://www.britannica.com/topic/Shariah

Deuraseh, N., & Abu Talib, M. (2005). Mental health in Islamic medical tradition. *The International Medical Journal*, *4*(2), 76–79.

Ergin, N. (2015). Healing by design? An experiential approach to early modern Ottoman hospital architecture. *Turkish Historical Review*, *6*(1), 1–37.

Gabr, A. H. (1992). *The influence of traditional Muslim beliefs on medieval religious architecture: Of the Bahri Mamluk period.* Ph.D., The University of Edinburgh,

United Kingdom Retrieved December 12, 2021, from https://www.proquest.com/docview/301511994?parentSessionId=VNmlUljc6rCQ58luLCU3xJlSwz1%2FwBOJ4TYg3uVXgjU%3D&pq-origsite=primo&

Gillis, K., & Gatersleben, B. (2015). A review of psychological literature on the health and wellbeing benefits of biophilic design. *Buildings*, *5*(3), Article 3.

Hamlin, T. F. (1940). Architecture of hospitals. *Pencil Points*, *21*(11), 711–720.

Healthcare: Healing by Design. (2013). *Construction Week*, 2013, June 4. https://www.constructionweekonline.com/projects-tenders/article-22693-healthcare-healing-by-design

Horsburgh, C. R. (1995). Healing by design. *New England Journal of Medicine*, *333*(11), 735–740. https://doi.org/10.1056/NEJM199509143331117

Ibn Abī Uṣaybiʿah, A. I. A.-Q. (1882). *Uyūn al-anbāʾ fī ṭabaqāt al-aṭibbā [The Best Account of the C/asses of Physicians]* (Vol. 2). Early Arabic Printed Books-BL: Science and History. https://tinyurl.gale.com/tinyurl/EPFSY5

Ibn Qadi Bi'albak, B.-D. (2006). In A. F. A. R. Hanun & Y. Sabbagh (Eds.), *Mufarrih an-nafs ma yaglibu al-farah wa-'s-surur min al-atima wa-'l-adwiya wa-'l-angam wa-'l-utur [The Delighter of the Soul]*. Dar al-Kutub al-Ilmiya.

Ikhwān al-Ṣafā'. (1984). *Al-Risālah al-jāmi'ah: Tāj Rasā'il Ikhwān al-Ṣafā wa-Khullān al-Wafā [Epistles of the Brethren of Purity and Loyal Friends]* (al-Ṭab'ah 2). Dār al-Andalus.

Johnson, M. L. (2015). The embodied meaning of architecture. In *Mind in Architecture*. The MIT Press. https://doi.org/10.7551/mitpress/10318.003.0004

Keshavarzi, H., Ali, B. (2019). Islamic Perspectives on Psychological and Spiritual Well-Being and Treatment. In: Moffic, H., Peteet, J., Hankir, A., Awaad, R. (eds) *Islamophobia and Psychiatry*. Springer, Cham. https://doi-org.stanford.idm.oclc.org/10.1007/978-3-030-00512-2_4

Makdisi, George. (1984). *The Rise Of Colleges: Institutions Of Learning In Islam And The West*. Edinburgh University Press.

McClary, R. (2021). Dar Al-Shifaʾ Or Bimaristān? Islāmic hospitals of damascus, Sivas, and Cairo in the twelfth and thirteenth centuries. In: Gharipour, Mohammad (ed) *Health And Architecture: The History of spaces of healing and Care in Pre-Modern Era*. Bloomsbury Publishing Plc.

McIntosh, J., Marques, B., & Jenkin, G. (2022). The role of courtyards within acute mental health wards: Designing with recovery in mind. *International Journal of Environmental Research and Public Health*, *19*(18). https://doi.org/10.3390/ijerph191811414

Mohamed, Y. (1996). *Fitrah: The Islāmic Concept of Human Nature*. Ta-Ha Publishers.

Nasr, S. H. (1987). *Islāmic art and Spirituality*. State University of New York Press.

Nasr, S. H. (2010). *Islam in the modern world: Challenged by the West, threatened by fundamentalism, keeping faith with tradition* (1st ed.). HarperOne/HarperCollins.

Pallasmaa, J. (2012). *The Eyes of the Skin: Architecture and the Senses* (3rd ed.). Wiley.

Ragab, A. (2015). *The Medieval Islāmic Hospital: Medicine, Religion, and Charity*. Cambridge University Press. https://doi.org/10.1017/CBO9781316271797

Rubin, H. (1998). Status report: An investigation to determine whether the built environment affects patients' medical outcomes. *Journal of Healthcare Design : Proceedings from the... Symposium on Healthcare Design. Symposium on Healthcare Design, 10*. https://pubmed.ncbi.nlm.nih.gov/10539237/

Sam Debartolo (Director). (2019, October 27). *Juhani Pallasmaa Interview 2019*. https://www.youtube.com/watch?v=0SWY75kxxe0

Speaks, J. (2021). Theories of meaning. In E. N. Zalta (Ed.), *The Stanford Encyclopedia of Philosophy* (Spring ed.). https://plato.stanford.edu/archives/spr2021/entries/meaning/

Sullivan, L. H. (1896). The tall office building artistically considered: I. Ii. Iii. *Lippincott's Monthly Magazine*, 1886–1915, 403.

Saheeh International. (n.d.). *English Translation of the Meaning of the Holy Qur'ān*. Conveying Islāmic Message Society.

Thoma, M. V., Mewes, R., & Nater, U. M. (2018). Preliminary evidence: The stress-reducing effect of listening to water sounds depends on somatic complaints: A randomised trial. *Medicine (Baltimore)*, *97*(8), e9851–e9851. https://doi.org/10.1097/MD.0000000000009851

Ulrich, R. S. (1984). View through a window may influence recovery from surgery. *Science*, *224*(4647), 420–421. https://doi.org/10.1126/science.6143402

Ulrich, R. S., Zimring, C., Zhu, X., DuBose, J., Seo, H.-B., Choi, Y.-S., Quan, X., & Joseph, A. (2008). A review of the research literature on evidence-based healthcare design. *HERD*, *1*(3), 61–125. https://doi.org/10.1177/193758670800100306

Ulrich, R., Zimring, C., Quan, X., Joseph, A., & Choudhary, R. (2004). *The Role of the Physical Environment in the Hospital of the 21st Century*. The Center for Health Design.

Umar, F. A.-A. ((2002)). The perceptible and the unseen: The Qur'ānic conception of man's relationship to god and realities beyond human perception. In S. J. Palmer (Ed.), *Mormons and Muslims: Spiritual Foundations and Modern Manifestations* (pp. 209–64). Religious Studies Center, Brigham Young University.

6 The Maristān Blueprint

A Model for Holistic Care

Merve Nursoy-Demir, Fatima Alemam and Rania Awaad

Introduction

Maristāns stood as shining exemplars for mental healthcare during the mediaeval period and left behind a legacy that inspires us today. In previous chapters, we have highlighted the establishment (Chapters 1 and 2), features (Chapters 2, 3, and 5), operations (Chapter 3), and maintenance (Chapters 3 and 4) of the maristāns. Still, an important question remains: do these mediaeval marvels contain some practical value for the mental healthcare field today? In this chapter, we attempt to provide a blueprint of the maristān model of holistic care and discuss its applicability to the contemporary clinical practice of Islāmic Psychology (IP). To commence, we must note that the *niyyah* (intention) behind building a maristān is at the root of its effectiveness in delivering *shifā'* (healing).

Intention: The Islāmic Grounding for the Maristān Model of Care

The success of maristāns as one of the hallmarks of the Islāmic civilisation likely lies in its implementation of two central Islāmic teachings: *ikhlāṣ* (sincerity) in intention and *iḥsān* (excellence) in practice. Muslims believe that the success of any action depends on one's intentions (Al-Bukhârî, 1). Hence, the principle of *ikhlāṣ* likely directed a sense of purpose for maristān's founders, who aimed to provide healing for many generations. Likewise, the principle of *iḥsān* inspired innovative design, exceptional clinical care, and ongoing maintenance of these institutions. According to the Islāmic practice of making an intention prior to taking action, each Maristan's waqf documents outlined the explicit intentionality behind their inception, oftentimes showcasing the founder's earnest hopes that God may accept their healing center and make it beneficial (see Chapters 1 and 2). Furthermore, shared features across time and space (see Chapters 2, 3, and 5) support the idea of a standardised, shared intention of holistic healing in these institutions.

As such, the first lesson in establishing a modern maristān is for its founders and IP clinicians practising within its walls to set a sincere intention prior

DOI: 10.4324/9781003329589-6

to delivering any therapeutic services. The *ikhlāṣ* of the clinician is the seed that sprouts the clinical outcome. Accordingly, a firm *niyyah* grounded in Islāmic phenomenology, as in the case of the maristāns' establishment and maintenance, is expected to spiritually transform the therapeutic space into an effective healing space, strengthen the therapeutic relationship, and direct the therapeutic process towards healing. Guiding questions for setting this *niyyah* should include the following: what are the telos of the clinical intervention? What are the personal motivations of the clinician when delivering this service? When answers to such fundamental questions align with Islāmic principles, the success and efficacy of the clinical work is expected to multiply, not only in this world but in the hereafter, as well, according to the Islāmic worldview (*The Qur'ān*, 5:9). This, we argue, is the essence of IP practice: a deep regard for the intentionality behind one's actions coupled with excellence in clinical care.

Multiplexity in Treatment: Targeting the Whole Person

The multiplex, or multi-pronged, approach used in maristāns to define symptoms, examine patients, and execute interventions (see Chapter 4) differentiates it from the fragmented approach of modern psychology. Approaching the whole patient from a comprehensive lens by considering their body, mind, and soul greatly shaped how physicians diagnosed and treated illnesses in the maristāns historically. As such, while examining mental health conditions, physicians took into account the interconnected physiological, psychological, cognitive, social, and spiritual aspects of the patient. Most modern mental healthcare providers could benefit from acquiring a similar holistic approach due to the fractured nature of understanding and treating the self.

Post-modernity has led to the artificial compartmentalisation of sciences that did not plague pre-modern societies, including the societies of prominent Muslim thinkers and scholars. Although we have only recently recognised the many factors that impact health and disease, the practice of modern psychiatry overarchingly focuses on treating patients at the biological/neuropharmacological level, ignoring key aspects such as one's environment and spirituality. Meanwhile, modern psychotherapy targets an individual's psychology in a vacuum, severed from their community and collective reality. (Harrington, 2019). In stark contrast, the maristān model of care treats the root causes of a patient's psychological problems by holistically addressing their intertwined external (e.g., family, society, geography, living conditions, hygiene, social circles) and internal (e.g., biological health, spiritual state, and mindset) components.This Interconnectedness and interpenetration of all aspects of a patient's wellbeing as witnessed the maristan model of care is a direct reflection of Islam's multiplex tradition.

Islāmic Paradigm of Psychology as the Baseline

In addition to its theoretical multiplexity, at its core, the maristān model of healing is God-centric. Therefore, a patient's vertical connection with the Divine and the metaphysical realm precedes all other relationships. From an Islāmic perspective, a clinician must focus on a patient's relationship with God while implementing therapeutic interventions to support their complete recovery and well-being. From this framework of healing, we may define psychopathology as 'a disorder of perception, consciousness, and intentionality...which impedes... [the] preservation and facilitation of religion, intellect, and life/health: three of the primary purposes of Divine Law (*maqāṣid al-sharīʿah*)' (Yusuf & al-Akiti, 2022, p. 177). Applying such a deeply spiritual perspective to clinical practice may deepen the therapeutic relationship and effectiveness of interventions.

An application of this multiplex perspective expands and enhances the clinician's role, the client's potential, and their therapeutic relationship. The potential of the client is not limited to removing suffering associated with one's daily functioning; instead, it is to know God (*The Qurʾān*, 51:56). Therefore, we must consider spirituality and metaphysics in the therapeutic space to best understand the client's conditions and effectively work towards their betterment.

In addition to incorporating a holistic, God-centric approach to understanding human nature, current IP practitioners must broaden their perspective beyond conventional psychotherapy frameworks like Cognitive-Behavioural Therapy (CBT), Acceptance and Commitment Therapy (ACT), psychodynamic, or other therapies that neglect central aspects of the human being (such as their soul; Keshavarzi et al. 2020). Modern IP scholars (Merter, 2008; 2014; Rothman & Coyle, 2018; Yusuf & al-Akiti, 2022) suggest that acquiring a God-centred viewpoint when treating clients may allow practitioners to overcome the reductionistic, uniplex nature of modern psychotherapy methods.

The Clinician and Treatment Team

Based on the maristān model of care, a practitioner with training in multiple specialisations (e.g., a medical doctor with additional training in nutrition, acupuncture, and herbal medicine) or a multidisciplinary treatment team should plan and implement clinical interventions comprehensively. This multidisciplinary team should include one preliminary healer (i.e., therapist) working in consultation with a primary care physician, psychiatrist, dietician, religious consultant (e.g., hospital chaplain), and social worker. The interactive nature of a multidisciplinary team gives the therapist a fuller picture, enabling the integration of various research fields and, consequently, the administration of effective interventions in psychotherapy. To reflect this need, niche fields like psychoneuroendocrine immunology (PNEI) recently emerged to explore the endocrine system's mediating effects on stress affecting mental health illnesses (Bottaccioli et al., 2021; Feinstein & Church, 2010; Steinberg et al., 2015). Overall health, including regular blood, hormone, and genetic tests, should be consulted by primary care physicians to better understand and target the issues at hand. Similarly, the addition of a religious consultant and social worker to a patient's care team may help focus much needed attention on the spiritual and social aspects of the treatment plan, respectively (Timmins et al., 2018).

In addition to the multidisciplinary nature of the care provided in historical maristāns, two crucial characteristics of their treatment team serve as a blueprint for IP clinicians today: their virtuous personalities and positive bedside manners. The maristāns of the past set a standard for an inclusive and altruistic treatment team (see Chapters 3 and 4). The explicit criteria of *akẖlāq* (i.e., virtue and morality) served as an expectation of the care team and a primary requirement for employment in Islāmic hospitals. A team's *akẖlāq* was not only expected while administering professional care but also in their personal lives (Altıntaş, 2022; Ünver, 1939). Such a unique emphasis on virtuous behaviour differentiated Islāmic medicine in its humane approach and was crucial to the maristāns' medical and administrative success (Dols, 1992; Mitha, 2020).

The maristān model of care sets an essential blueprint for how clinicians should focus on personal virtuous growth as much as, if not more than, their professional development, as the competence of the IP clinician is directly associated with their moral maturity. Therefore, current-day clinicians should prioritise their spirituality through self-cleansing and self-improvement practices, such as *tazkiyah* (purification), *takẖliyah* (emptying), *murāqabah* (inspection), and *muḥāsabah* (examination) of the self. Another recommendation based on this historical model of care would be the spiritual preparation of clinicians prior to working with their clients. For example, clinicians should make *wuḍū'* (ablution) before therapy sessions, pray for their clients, and practice *ḏhikr* (remembrance of God) with the intention of preparing themselves to serve their clients. Through these practices, the IP clinician can improve their presence as a clean mirror (a spiritual motif denoting the clinician's role as a reflection of their client; Dawud, 1984) and as a spiritually uplifted guide.

These practices also consider the clinician's personal Islāmic practices as a relevant aspect of the therapeutic practise. Bringing the clinician's inner state, morality, and spirituality into the psychotherapeutic process as active components may be controversial in current clinical practice. Nevertheless, it deserves attention, especially since empirical evidence shows that the quality of the therapeutic relationship itself (Baier et al., 2020; Norcross & Lambert, 2019; Weck et al., 2015) and the personal characteristics of the clinician (Heinonen et al., 2012; Heinonen & Nissen-Lie, 2020) may influence the success of therapeutic processes regardless of the specific methods used. Hence, neither psychotherapy nor healing in a broader sense is mechanical or technical, as was understood by our Muslim predecessors centuries ago (Ünver, 1939).

An Openness to Alternative Ways of Healing

In modern psychology, numerous changes have occurred in the approved methods of treatment, scientific measurements, and modalities of diagnosing and treating mental health issues (Fleuridas & Krafcik, 2019). For instance, researchers once used to view experimental designs with randomised controlled trials as the most reliable measure of research; however, current trends in research encourage the use of qualitative methods, allowing for less sterile and more diverse methodologies (Rennie et al., 2002; Willig, 2019). Likewise, in clinical practice, recently developed psychotherapy methods, such as Mindfulness-Based Cognitive Therapy (MBCT), Acceptance and Commitment Therapy (ACT), Dialectical Behavioural Therapy (DBT), and Eye Movement Desensitisation and Reprocessing (EMDR), are slowly replacing more traditional techniques such as CBT (Hayes & Hofmann, 2021; Rydberg & Machado, 2020; Soares et al., 2020). Reflecting the changes in research and practices of modern psychology, IP practitioners should cultivate an openness to new methodologies, including more holistic methods used historically, while exploring newly emerging tools. The maristān model of care advocates for an open approach to novel clinical practices, enabling a wide range of applied treatment tools to provide truly integrative care. Accordingly, the model advises that practitioners stay open to alternative tools in clinical practice and utilise complementary healing methods available beyond the field's current boundaries. Examples include incorporating temperament (*mīzāj*) theories, sound therapies, or IP-based self-help tools. This would require a multidisciplinary approach to bridge historical mental health treatment modalities used in the maristāns with modern clinical practice without dismissing historical approaches as outdated or blindly accepting them as 'Islāmic'.

For example, modern IP practitioners should explore and incorporate sound therapy, as found in historical maristāns (Chapter 4). Sounds of nature, such as bird songs and water sounds, and Qur'ānic recitation using the *maqāmāt* (melodic modes), were regularly used in maristāns when treating psychiatric patients (Awaad & Demir, 2023). Modern literature establishes music therapy as an effective, evidence-based discipline that positively impacts psychological well-being (Hillecke et al., 2005). While the permissibility of instrumental music is a controversial issue in Islāmic law, using natural sounds and human voices is usually permissible (Agrawal et al., 2022; Egypt's Dar Al-Ifta, 2013). Hence, clinicians should consider utilising Islāmically permissible melodies for holistic healing.

Some of the current movements in mental healthcare are reviving a focus on whole-person treatment (Fleuridas & Krafcik, 2019; Gilbert & Kirby, 2019), with emerging studies demonstrating the effectiveness of holistic care. Decades-long research shows that the relationships between nature and nurture, genetics and the environment, and the body and mind are considerably more interactive and complex than once believed (Rutten et al., 2013; Smeeth et al., 2021). As such, well-documented phenomena, such as experience-dependent neuroplasticity (Hanson, 2017; Joja, 2013) and epigenetics (Schiele et al., 2020), have driven clinicians to creatively integrate the multiple dimensions of human existence into therapy (Fleuridas & Krafcik, 2019; Gilbert & Kirby, 2019; Latorre, 2000; Sultanoff, 1997; Walsh, 2011).

By implementing the maristān model of treatment, modern clinical practice can be pushed even further towards holistic healing in its most faithful sense: in ways that explore the spiritual potential of the person and do not empirically reduce the definition of personhood, illness, and, ultimately, health (Yusuf & al-Akiti, 2022)

The Healing Environment: Physical and Metaphysical Spaces of Holistic Care

Historically, a maristān's chief physician, accompanied by the hospital staff (Chapters 3 and 4), delivered direct patient care. In addition, numerous hospital design elements (e.g., the physical setting, administrative structure, attitudes, food, and service delivery) accompanied the healing process as indirect agents (Chapters 4 and 5) that concomitantly healed a patient's senses, mind, and soul. Historical maristans bore witness to the synthesis of aesthetics without sacrificing functionality.

Physical Space of Healing

The maristan healing method specifically targeted each of the five senses to promote comprehensive healing (see Chapter 5). Māristāns contained lush foliage alongside aesthetic, symbolic architecture that played a crucial role in visually filling patients' hearts with *shifā'*. Birds chirping in the gardens, the gentle sound of running water from the central fountain, and soothing musical tones reverberating in the courtyard utilised the auditory healing channel as part of the patient's mental health care. Treatment in the maristāns also targeted patients' olfactory sense by intentionally curating flower gardens filled with lavender and basil and the use of *bukhūr* (incense) that would waft through the hospital. Customised nutritious meals and carefully prescribed drugs healed patients through their sense of taste. Lastly, wearing and sleeping on high-quality linens, intentional cleansing sessions in the *ḥammām* (bathhouse), and care from compassionate guardians ensured that patients were also healed via their sense of touch. As such, all five of a patient's senses must be engaged as part of their treatment plan in order for a proper revival and implementation of the maristan healing model to occur.

Furthermore, IP practitioners aiming to implement the maristān model of holistic care should establish a centrally located, easily accessible clinic (such as near a Muslim community centre or mosque) to avoid unintentional exclusion and further stigmatisation of those seeking mental healthcare. These therapeutic spaces should opt for moderate sized centres to encourage a sense of comfort, contrary to most contemporary hospitals that may foster a sense of feeling overwhelmed due to their large size (Ergin, 2015). The clinical setting should be easy to navigate with a simple layout, whether the clinic is housed within its own independent building or a shared office space. Additionally, the clinic should prioritise security and privacy, for example, ensuring patient quarters have closed doors, separated rooms, and curtains. Lastly, the area would ideally contain Islāmic architectural and geometrical structural elements for their outward aesthetic and inward symbolic connotations (similar to those in the International Medical Center Hospital; "*International*", n.d.).

A modern, maristān-inspired clinic that is designed from a biophilic lens should incorporate natural living elements such as leafage, flowers, water fountains, and song birds. Moreover, integrating natural elements inside the clinic could include the use of earth tones, natural materials (e.g., wood, marble, stone, glass, and bamboo), and calming scents of lavender, basil, and rose (Chapter 5). The maristān should also be spacious, with ventilation that brings in fresh air and feature large windows that bring in natural light. Ideally, the layout would include a central courtyard to promote connection with the natural world (Naderi & Shin, 2008).

It is astounding that historically, the majority of the maristāns across space and time incorporated most if not all of the elements of the biophilic design as defined by the field today, including fresh air, daylight, plants, animals, landscape, forms and shapes, patterns and geometries, materials, texture, colour, refuge, and order (Zhong et al., 2022). In addition to biophilic design elements, research emerging from fields such as neuroaesthetics (Chatterjee et al., 2021; Nanda et al., 2009), ecotherapy (Kahveci & Göker, 2019), and colour psychology (Birren, 2016) provide additional support for the design elements once used in historical maristāns. Emerging literature in the field of Neuroaesthetics emphasises the importance of utilising the healing effects of visual space on human psychology, especially in healthcare settings (Nanda et al., 2009), by incorporating corridors filled with greenery similar to those found in the historical maristāns. Similarly, ecotherapy emphasises the positive effects of interacting with nature on patient well-being (Wilson et al., 2009). These newly emerging scientific findings continue to align with the healing elements that were once employed in the maristāns historically and must be taken into account by IP practioners aiming to implement the maristan model of healing today.

Metaphysical Space of Healing

The metaphysical dimension of a space is a crucial characteristic of maristāns that is currently missing from most hospital designs today. Maristāns curated this dimension through two primary components: embedding physical structures with subtle yet symbolic reminders that connect humans to their Creator (see Chapter 5) and purifying the space to invite ethereal agents of tranquillity, namely, angels.

Regarding the first component, the Muslims who established and worked in the maristāns were acutely aware of the main ingredient that can genuinely bring ease to human beings: an uninterrupted connection to the Divine. Therefore, the architectural design of historical maristāns promoted metaphysical elements of *Tawhîd* in line with the reminder of the Qur'ānic verse, 'Unquestionably, by the remembrance of Allāh hearts are assured' (*The Qur'ān*, 13:28; see Chapter 5). Regarding the second component of the metaphysical dimension, maristāns sought to attract the angelic presence—which Muslims believe to have a substantial positive influence on humans (Riyad As-Salihin, 1985). This was achieved through the maristans' clean, fragrantly scented, and spiritually uplifting atmosphere, the three essential ingredients for attractive angelic presence. The Qur'ān describes the importance of angelic presence, stating that each person has guardian angels 'before and behind him who protect him by the decree of Allāh' (13:11).

Established using this Islāmically inspired metaphysical perspective, the maristān model of holistic care also suggests that a place of healing must provide reminders of one's vertical connection to the Divine through the symbolism of its art and architecture. The symbolic message of *Tawhîd*, as commonly found in the maristān's architecture, may be utilised in contemporary IP clinics to uplift the patients' spirits. The practical outcome of this metaphysical understanding is to designate a clinical space that is both physically and spiritually uplifting, clean, naturally scented, and ornamented with Islāmic art and geometrical designs as gentle reminders to the soul and invitations to draw in a stronger angelic presence.

Sustainable Financing

Financial independence was another critical characteristic that led to the maristāns' prolonged success in delivering continuous state-of-the-art healthcare services. Every maristān showcased in this book (see Chapter 3) had continuous, sufficient, and well-protected sources of income through endowments that were managed by carefully selected trustees. Additionally, a system of checks and balances was instituted to ensure the proper handling of funds, such that judges could remove the responsibility of handling funds from the managers if they deemed them unfit due to irresponsible expenditure. In order to create accessible and sustainable clinical initiatives in the field of IP today, it is imperative to learn from the financial management of the maristāns, considering that all of them operated for centuries and long outlived their founders. Indeed, modern mental healthcare financing models can benefit from the financial models and techniques used in these historical and immensely impactful institutions.

Modern Mental Healthcare Funding

There are significant limitations in the availability and affordability of clinical care for psychiatric illnesses in affluent countries such as the US and the UK (Abrams, 2023; Kotera et al., 2022; Miles, 2016). Residents of Egypt (Okasha et al., 2022), Malaysia (Raaj et al., 2021), and Turkey ("World", n.d.) face similar challenges to those living in the UK and the US regarding a rise in mental health illness needs and overstretched or unavailable service providers ("WHO-AIMS", 2006; Yap et al., 2020; "Turkey", 2022).

The global COVID-19 pandemic revealed that the mental healthcare system in the US—one of the world's wealthiest countries—suffers from severe disparity, affordability, and accessibility issues (Abrams, 2023; Schubert, 2022). Similarly, current mental health services in the UK raise concerns about quality, sustainability, and accessibility despite efforts to increase the diversity and accessibility of mental health services throughout the country (Abrams, 2023; Kotera et al., 2022). The accessibility of mental health practitioners in both the US (Butryn et al., 2017) and the UK (Peter et al., 2005) is also a significant issue. More than half of the individuals identified with a mental illness in the US did not get help in 2020 (Schubert, 2022). The financial set-up of the US healthcare system also requires patients to pay excessive bills for mental health treatments, in addition to their insurance coverage and preventive care costs. In the UK, regardless of the free mental health coverage through the government-funded National Health Service (NHS), people who sought help had to endure long waitlists ("Autism," 2019; Punton et al., 2022) and there was a significant decrease in the availability of clinical services as 13% of mental health staff quit from 2021 to 2022 (Campbell, 2023). The problem partly stems from reduced funding for mental health providers and, simultaneously, an increased demand for mental healthcare (Mahase, 2023). According to the House of Commons Committee of Public Accounts, high turnover rates from those working in the NHS's mental health task force augmented long wait times for patients post-pandemic in the UK.

Underrepresented communities, such as Muslims, have even less access to culturally congruent care (often in the form of Muslim therapists). If they do find a suitable clinician, the clinic may not accept their insurance, shrinking an already small pool of appropriate providers (Butryn et al., 2017). At steadily decreasing rates since 2005, psychiatrists have one of the lowest rates of accepting insurance in the US due to various issues with the insurance system, such as restrictions on their scope of practice, low payout rates, and limited time with patients (Bishop, 2014). A solution is urgently needed as the gap widens between the increasing demand for mental healthcare services and the need for more clinicians. For the patient, the financial burden imposed by these expenses extends into a psychological burden that exacerbates their need for care. Unfortunately, the prospect of incurring debt likely hinders seeking treatment for those who need it most (University, 2021). Many of these chronic issues stem from placing the financial burden of care on those seeking help and practitioners who genuinely want to provide aid.

Addressing the Financial Gaps in Modern Mental Healthcare by Implementing the Maristān Model

A potential pathway to improve mental healthcare and provide quality, accessible, and affordable mental health services is to adopt the philanthropic, community-centred mechanisms utilised historically by maristāns. Today, Muslim communities in non-Muslim countries, such as the US and UK, are accustomed to financially establishing and sustaining religious institutions. Most of the *masājid* in the US, the UK, and other places in Europe were established as collaborative, philanthropic community projects. Similar initiatives should be encouraged to develop Muslim mental healthcare clinics that utilise tax-deductible, non-profit, governmental policies.

There are three forms of philanthropic income within the Islāmic charitable model that was applied to maristāns and other community-centred projects historically: (1) zakat (annual religiously obligatory donations), (2) *ṣadaqah* (i.e., voluntary donations), and (3) *awqāf* (one-time, self-sustaining voluntary endowments; see Chapter 3 for more information). Zakat is an obligatory yearly payment of 2.5% on all assets (including cash, stocks, livestock, and gold), and it can facilitate the redistribution of wealth for various community-centred projects, such as mental health clinics. Researchers estimate that anywhere from $200 billion to $1 trillion USD exists in the annual global zakat pool (Fahlefi et al., 2019; Rehman & Pickup, 2018). This 2.5% on accumulated assets is remarkably equitable: regardless of one's income, if a person is under financial strain (i.e., is barely able to cover their living expenses and has no savings of any form), they will not be required to pay zakat, and indeed, may be eligible to receive it (Fahlefi et al., 2019). The same applies to those with significantly accumulated wealth, who are required to donate 2.5% yearly, regardless of the legalities of their earnings if they possess accumulated wealth of any kind (with some exceptions). While Muslim scholars recommend focusing zakat funds on local organisations and individuals first, as seen with the establishments of the historical maristāns (Chapter 2), almost a fourth of American Muslims' zakat funds international organisations (Shariq et al., 2022). Studying the historical maristāns allows us to reorient modern Muslims' zakat to fund more local needs, such as local mental health organisations.

Compared to tax structures set up by Western governments today, which are primarily determined based on income and not assets, zakat is less demanding and more lucrative. The second form of philanthropic income within the Islāmic model, *ṣadaqah*, is not to be underestimated. Despite being minorities, both UK (Habib & Roberts, 2023) and American (Siddiqui & Wasif, 2021) Muslims are significant contributors to charitable causes compared to other religious donors.

The final form of Islāmic charity, *awqāf*, is of considerable interest for establishing and sustaining community needs, such as mental health services. As discussed at length in Chapter 3, donating endowed properties, agricultural lands, or stocks and similar sources that produce a steady source of income (such as those donated for mosques in the US and the UK) can unlock the revival of everlasting endowments that empower community services like maristāns for the foreseeable future. For example, one of the historical maristāns, Bīmaristān al-Sayyidah, was waqf-funded with 600 dirhams per month during its construction and sustained for around 250 dirhams a month (Thābit ibn Sinān as quoted by Ragab, 2015).

Although such an understanding of endowment for mental health services specifically may seem out of reach, a few non-profit organisations focusing on mental health for Muslims are funded through community support. One example is the Maristān Clinic—using the historical maristāns as its namesake—a recently launched IP and Muslim mental health organisation based in California. By integrating its first therapy office within the communal space of a masjid, Maristān models its care after the historical *kulliyyah* complexes. Furthermore, Maristan's clinic provides multiple avenues to fund its services while providing its less affluent clients with several financial aid opportunities that significantly reduce treatment fees. Other grassroots, community-driven organisations implementing these models in the West are emerging (e.g., The National Waqf Organization). Like their Islāmic predecessors, these promising buds based on the rooted revival of Islāmic charitable frameworks will hopefully blossom in due time into fully self-sustaining service providers for the mental health needs of modern Muslim communities today.

Conclusion

The historical maristāns provide the necessary blueprint for the rooted revival of Islāmic heritage in designing a modern IP clinic or centre by first establishing a strong foundation through an Islāmically rooted intention, guiding the actions of founders and practitioners of the clinic to serve patients with excellence. By utilising the maristan model of care, modern IP clinics can aim to approach patient care holistically by integrating historically utilised healing techniques with novel psychotherapeutic approaches where applicable. This chapter highlighted key features of the intentional use of space, nature, and symbolism common in most historical maristāns. Elucidating the self-sustaining financial structures and affordable care systems that historically funded the care of patients regardless of their socioeconomic backgrounds can help encourage a modern revival of such financing options. In conclusion, whether through their bio-psycho-social-spiritual conceptualisation of mental health, collaborative and investigative clinical research system, or their strong emphasis on the importance of the provider-patient relationship, mental health treatments in maristāns between the 8th and 19th centuries set a strong precedent for holistic and whole-person healing. In conclusion, implementing the maristan healing model is a necessity in order to heal our modern fragmented mental healthcare systems and worthy of reviving in the modern era.

References

Abrams, Z. (2023, January 1). Kids' mental health is in crisis. Here's what psychologists are doing to help. *Monitor on Psychology*, *54*(1). https://www.apa.org/monitor/2023/01/trends-improving-youth-mental-health

Abū Dāwūd, S. (n.d.). *Regarding sincere counsel and protection.* sunnah.com - sayings and teachings of Prophet Muḥammad (ﷺ). https://sunnah.com/abudawud:4918

Agrawal, A., Sutar, R., & Jallapally, A. (Eds.). (2022). *Music in Health and Diseases*. IntechOpen.

Ahmadi, M., Shirafkan, H., & Mozaffarpur, S. A. (2023). Assessment of the diagnostic methods of Mizaj in Persian Medicine: A systematic review. *Diagnostics*, *13*(5), 818. https://doi.org/10.3390/diagnostics13050818

Al-Bukhârî, M. (n.d.). *How the Divine Revelation started being revealed to Allāh's Messenger.* sunnah.com - sayings and teachings of Prophet Muḥammad (ﷺ). https://sunnah.com/bukhari:1

Altıntaş, A. (2022). Anadolu Tibbi Nedir-Neden Önemlidir? *Anadolu Tıbbı Dergisi*, 1(1), 1. https://dergipark.org.tr/en/pub/anadolutibbi/issue/73485/1207955

An-Nasā'i, A. (n.d.). *Regarding sincere counsel and protection.* sunnah.com - sayings and teachings of Prophet Muhammad (ﷺ).

Awaad, R., & Nursoy-Demir, M. (2023). Melodies in the hospital courtyard: A comparative history of Ottoman music therapy in the early modern period (c. 1400–1800). *The Arts in Psychotherapy*, *86*, 102092. https://doi.org/10.1016/j.aip.2023.102092

Baier, A. L., Kline, A. C., & Feeny, N. C. (2020). Therapeutic alliance as a mediator of change: A systematic review and evaluation of research. *Clinical Psychology Review*, *82*, 101921. https://doi.org/10.1016/j.cpr.2020.101921

Birren, F. (2016). *Color Psychology and Color Therapy: A Factual Study of the Influence of Color on Human Life*. Pickle Partners Publishing.

Bishop, T. F., Press, M. J., Keyhani, S., & Pincus, H. A. (2014). Acceptance of insurance by psychiatrists and the implications for access to mental health care. *JAMA Psychiatry*, *71*(2), 176–181. doi:10.1001/jamapsychiatry.2013.2862

Bottaccioli, F., Bottaccioli, A. G., Marzola, E., Longo, P., Minelli, A., & Abbate-Daga, G. (2021). Nutrition, exercise, and stress management for treatment and prevention of psychiatric disorders. *A Narrative Review Psychoneuroendocrineimmunology-Based Endocrines*, *2*(3), 3. https://doi.org/10.3390/endocrines2030022

Butryn, T., Bryant, L., Marchionni, C., & Sholevar, F. (2017). The shortage of psychiatrists and other mental health providers: Causes, current state, and potential solutions. *International Journal of Academic Medicine*, *3*(1), 5. https://doi.org/10.4103/IJAM.IJAM_49_17

Campbell, D. (2023, February 9). Millions with mental health needs not seeking NHS help, Watchdog says. *The Guardian*. https://www.theguardian.com/society/2023/feb/09/millions-with-mental-health-needs-not-seeking-nhs-help-watchdog-says

Center, I. M. (n.d.). International Medical Center Hospital. https://imc.med.sa/en

Chatterjee, A., Coburn, A., & Weinberger, A. (2021). The neuroaesthetics of architectural spaces. *Cognitive Processing*, *22*(S1), 115–120. https://doi.org/10.1007/s10339-021-01043-4

Dierks, Z. (2022). *Turkey: Problems with National Health Care System 2021*. Statista. (2022, November 28). https://www.statista.com/statistics/1272606/problems-with-national-health-care-system-in-turkey/

Dols, M. W. (1992). *Majnūn: The Madman in Medieval Islamic Society.* https://doi.org/10.1093/acprof:oso/9780198202219.001.0001

Egypt's Dar al-Iftaa. (2013, July 22). What is the ruling concerning music? *Egypt's Dar al-Ifta.* https://www.dar-alifta.org/en/fatwa/details/4866/what-is-the-ruling-concerning-music

Ergin, N. (2015). Healing by design? An experiential approach to early modern Ottoman hospital architecture. *Turkish Historical Review*, *6*(1), 1–37.

Fahlefi, R., Hasan, A., & Alimin, A. (2019). Management model of Zakat collection and its distribution for zakat agency / management model of Zakat collection and its distribution for Zakat Agency. *Uluslararası Ekonomi İşletme ve Politika Dergisi*, *3*(2), 171–182. https://doi.org/10.29216/ueip.561657

Feinstein, D., & Church, D. (2010). Modulating gene expression through psychotherapy: The contribution of noninvasive somatic interventions. *Review of General Psychology*, *14*(4), 283–295. https://doi.org/10.1037/a0021252

Fleuridas, C., & Krafcik, D. (2019). Beyond four forces: The evolution of psychotherapy. *SAGE Open*, *9*(1), 2158244018824492. https://doi.org/10.1177/2158244018824492

Gilbert, P., & Kirby, J. N. (2019). Building an integrative science for psychotherapy for the 21st century: Preface and introduction. *Psychology and Psychotherapy: Theory, Research and Practice*, *92*(2), 151–163. https://doi.org/10.1111/papt.12225

Habib, A., & Roberts, B. (2023). British Muslim charitable giving report II. *Muslim Charities Forum.* https://www.muslimcharitiesforum.org.uk/resources/british-muslim-charitable-giving-report-ii-the-impact-of-the-cost-of-living-crisis/

Hanson, R. (2017). Positive neuroplasticity: The neuroscience of mindfulness. In Loizzo, J., Wolf, E.J., & Neale, M. (Eds.), *Advances in Contemplative Psychotherapy: Accelerating Healing and Transformation* (1st ed.). Routledge. https://doi-org.stanford.idm.oclc.org/10.4324/9781315630045

Harrington A. (2019). *Mind Fixers: Psychiatry's Troubled Search for the Biology of Mental Illness.* W.W. Norton & Co. Inc.

Hayes, S. C., & Hofmann, S. G. (2021). "Third-wave" cognitive and behavioral therapies and the emergence of a process-based approach to intervention in psychiatry. *World Psychiatry*, *20*(3), 363–375. https://doi.org/10.1002/wps.20884

Heinonen, E., & Nissen-Lie, H. A. (2020). The professional and personal characteristics of effective psychotherapists: A systematic review. *Psychotherapy Research*, *30*(4), 417–432. https://doi.org/10.1080/10503307.2019.1620366

Heinonen, E., Lindfors, O., Laaksonen, M. A., & Knekt, P. (2012). Therapists' professional and personal characteristics as predictors of outcome in short- and long-term psychotherapy. *Journal of Affective Disorders*, *138*(3), 301–312. https://doi.org/10.1016/j.jad.2012.01.023

Hillecke, T., Nickel, A., & Bolay, H. V. (2005). Scientific perspectives on music therapy. *Annals of the New York Academy of Sciences*, *1060*(1), 271–282. https://doi.org/10.1196/annals.1360.020

Joja, D. O. (2013). *Learning experience and neuroplasticity–a shifting paradigm. 12*, 159–170. https://noema.crifst.ro/ARHIVA/2013_3_2.pdf

Kahveci, H., Göker, P. (2019). Mental health and wellbeing; Ecotherapy. *PERINTIS eJournal*, *12*(2), 108–12. https://www.set-science.com/manage/uploads/ISAS2019-FDAS_0040/SETSCI_ISAS2019-FDAS_0040_0037.pdf

Keshavarzi, H., Khan, F., Ali, B., & Awaad, R. (Eds.). (2020). *Applying Islamic principles to clinical mental health care: Introducing traditional Islamically integrated psychotherapy*. Routledge.

Kotera, Y., Harris, A., Raschbauer, J., & Gibson, A. (2022). Falling in a gap in mental health services in the UK: A perspective paper. *International Journal of Spa and Wellness*, *5*(1), 95–100. https://doi.org/10.1080/24721735.2021.2013649

Latorre, M. A. (2000). A holistic view of psychotherapy: Connecting mind, body, and spirit. *Perspectives in Psychiatric Care*, *36*(2), 67–68. https://www.proquest.com/docview/200790529/abstract/C437E92F6040428FPQ/1

Mahase, E. (2023). Government must get a "firmer grip" on mental health crisis, says watchdog. *BMJ*, p324. https://doi.org/10.1136/bmj.p324

Merter, M. (2008). *Dokuz Yüz Katlı İnsan. 10*. Kaknüs Yayınları.

Merter, M. (2014). *Psikolojinin üçüncü boyutu nefs psikolojisi ve rüyaların dili*. Kaknüs Yayınları.

Miles. (2016, May 17). *Mental Health: US vs UK*. Psych Central. https://psychcentral.com/lib/mental-health-us-vs-uk

Mitha, K. (2020). Conceptualising and addressing mental disorders amongst Muslim communities: Approaches from the Islāmic Golden Age. *Transcultural Psychiatry*, *57*(6), 763–774. https://doi.org/10.1177/1363461520962603

Naderi, J. R., & Shin, W.-H. (2008). Humane design for hospital landscapes: A case study in landscape architecture of a healing garden for nurses. *HERD: Health Environments Research & Design Journal*, *2*(1), 82–119. https://doi.org/10.1177/193758670800200112

Nanda, U., Pati, D., & McCurry, K. (2009). Neuroesthetics and healthcare design. *HERD: Health Environments Research & Design Journal*, *2*(2), 116–133. https://doi.org/10.1177/193758670900200210

Norcross, J. C., & Lambert, M. J. (Eds.). (2019). *Psychotherapy Relationships that Work: Vol. 1:* Evidence-Based Therapist Contributions. Oxford University Press.

Okasha, T., Rabie, M., Shaker, N. M., Mohsen, N., EL- Habiby, M., El-Gabry, D. A., Gaber, E., Ali, N., Ali, M., & Sayed, M. (2022). Mental health services in Egypt during the COVID-19 pandemic. *Middle East Current Psychiatry*, *29*(1), 102. https://doi.org/10.1186/s43045-022-00270-5

Parvizi, M. M., Nimrouzi, M., Pasalar, M., Salehi, A., Hajimonfarednejad, M., Amini, F., Mousavi Shirazi, R., & Rezaie, P. (2018). Association between personality types and temperament (Mizaj) based on Persian medicine. *Shiraz E-Medical Journal*, *19*(12). https://doi.org/10.5812/semj.68950

Punton, G., Dodd, A. L., & McNeill, A. (2022). 'You're on the waiting list': An interpretive phenomenological analysis of young adults' experiences of waiting lists within mental health services in the UK. *Plos One*, *17*(3), e0265542. https://doi.org/10.1371/journal.pone.0265542

Raaj, S., Navanathan, S., Tharmaselan, M., & Lally, J. (2021). Mental disorders in Malaysia: An increase in lifetime prevalence. *BJPsych International*, *18*(4), 97–99. https://doi.org/10.1192/bji.2021.4

Ragab, A. (2015). *The Medieval Islamic Hospital: Medicine, Religion, and Charity*. Cambridge University Press. https://doi.org/10.1017/CBO9781316271797

Rehman, A.A., & Pickup, F. (2018, September 7). *Zakat for the SDGs*. United Nations Development Programme. https://www.undp.org/blog/zakat-sdgs

Rennie, D. L., Watson, K. D., & Monteiro, A. M. (20020814). The rise of qualitative research in psychology. *Canadian Psychology/Psychologie Canadienne*, *43*(3), 179. https://doi.org/10.1037/h0086914

Riyad As-Salihin. (1985). Pakistan. Kazi Pub.

Rothman, A., & Coyle, A. (2018). Toward a framework for Islāmic psychology and psychotherapy: An Islāmic model of the soul. *Journal of Religion and Health*, *57*(5), 1731–1744. https://doi.org/10.1007/s10943-018-0651-x

Rutten, B. P. F., Hammels, C., Geschwind, N., Menne-Lothmann, C., Pishva, E., Schruers, K., van den Hove, D., Kenis, G., van Os, J., & Wichers, M. (2013). Resilience in mental health: Linking psychological and neurobiological perspectives. *Acta Psychiatrica Scandinavica*, *128*(1), 3–20. https://doi.org/10.1111/acps.12095

Rydberg, J. A., & Machado, J. (2020). Integrative psychotherapy and psychotherapy integration: The case of EMDR. *European Journal of Trauma & Dissociation*, *4*(3), 100165. https://doi.org/10.1016/j.ejtd.2020.100165

Saheeh International. (n.d.). *English translation of the meaning of the Holy Qur'ān. Conveying Islāmic Message Society.*

Schiele, M. A., Gottschalk, M. G., & Domschke, K. (2020). The applied implications of epigenetics in anxiety, affective and stress-related disorders—A review and synthesis on psychosocial stress, psychotherapy and prevention. *Clinical Psychology Review*, *77*, 101830. https://doi.org/10.1016/j.cpr.2020.101830

Schubert, S. (2022). *The grass is greener on the other side of the Ocean: Adopting foreign reforms to improve mental health care in the United States.* https://scholarship.shu.edu/cgi/viewcontent.cgi?article=2303&context=student_scholarship

Shariq Siddiqui, Micah A. Hughes, & Rafeel Wasif. (2022, December 14). How Muslim Americans meet their charitable obligations: 3 findings from New Research. *The Conversation*. https://theconversation.com/how-muslim-americans-meet-their-charitable-obligations-3-findings-from-new-research-180648#:~:text=Some%2025.3%25%20of%20the%20money,is%20sent%20abroad%20as%20remittances

Siddiqui, S., & Wasif, R. (2021). *Muslim American Giving 2021*. Muslim Philanthropy Initiative Lilly Family School of Philanthropy. https://scholarworks.iupui.edu/server/api/core/bitstreams/32235367-58a0-4155-b2bc-b1718ddf4216/content

Smeeth, D., Beck, S., Karam, E. G., & Pluess, M. (2021). The role of epigenetics in psychological resilience. *The Lancet Psychiatry*, *8*(7), 620–629. https://doi.org/10.1016/S2215-0366(20)30515-0

Soares, E. E., Thrall, J. N., Stephens, T. N., Rodriguez Biglieri, R., Consoli, A. J., & Bunge, E. L. (2020). Publication trends in psychotherapy: Bibliometric analysis of the past 5 decades. *American Journal of Psychotherapy*, *73*(3), 85–94. https://doi.org/10.1176/appi.psychotherapy.20190045

Steinberg, H., Kirkby, K. C., & Himmerich, H. (2015). The historical development of immunoendocrine concepts of psychiatric disorders and their therapy. *International Journal of Molecular Sciences*, *16*(12), Article 12. https://doi.org/10.3390/ijms161226136

Sultanoff, S. M. (1997). Treating the whole person: A holistic approach to psychotherapy. *The Humanistic Psychologist*, *25*(2), 126. https://doi.org/10.1080/08873267.1997.9986876

Timmins, F., Caldeira, S., Murphy, M., Pujol, N., Sheaf, G., Weathers, E., Whelan, J., & Flanagan, B. (2018). The role of the healthcare chaplain: A literature review.

Journal of Health Care Chaplaincy, *24*(3), 87–106. https://doi.org/10.1080/08854726.2017.1338048

Tiryaki, M. Z., & Bilgin Tiryaki, K. (2016). *İslam düşüncesinde mizaç teorileri* (1. basım: Ağustos 2016.). Nobel Akademik Yayıncılık.

University, S. (2021, October 6). Study finds medical debt is a double whammy for the poor. *Stanford News*. https://news.stanford.edu/2021/10/07/study-finds-medical-debt-double-whammy-poor/

Ünver, S. A. (1939). *400. Yıldönümü Dolayısıyla Haseki Hastanesi Tarihçesi*. Kader Basımevi.

Walsh, R. (2011). Lifestyle and mental health. *American Psychologist*, *66*, 579–592. https://doi.org/10.1037/a0021769

Weck, F., Grikscheit, F., Jakob, M., Höfling, V., & Stangier, U. (2015). Treatment failure in cognitive-behavioural therapy: Therapeutic alliance as a precondition for an adherent and competent implementation of techniques. *British Journal of Clinical Psychology*, *54*(1), 91–108. https://doi.org/10.1111/bjc.12063

WHO (2006). *WHO-AIMS Report on Mental Health System in (Egypt)*. WHO and Ministry of Health.

Willig, C. (2019). What can qualitative psychology contribute to psychological knowledge? *Psychological Methods*, *24*, 796–804. https://doi.org/10.1037/met0000218

Wilson, N., Ross, M., Lafferty, K., & Jones, R. (2009). A review of ecotherapy as an adjunct form of treatment for those who use mental health services. *Journal of Public Mental Health*, *7*(3), 23–35. https://doi.org/10.1108/17465729200800020

World Health Organization. (n.d.). *Supporting Turkish Mental Health Policy and Service Delivery*. World Health Organization. https://www.who.int/about/accountability/results/who-results-report-2020-mtr/country-story/2020/supporting-turkish-mental-health-policy-and-service-delivery#:~:text=According%20to%20the%20data%20of,56%20percent%20in%20five%20years

Yap, A., Daojuin, D., Jingqi, H., Sim, I., Wong, J., Firdaus, M. (2020). *Improving Accessibility and Availability of Mental Health Services in Malaysia*. Malaysian Medics International. https://static1.squarespace.com/static/5e477eb18ae6b644167d06ab/t/5effd4ec1ccde6142bad3e5e/1615358793330/Policy-2020-02+-+Mental+Health+Policy.pdf

Yusuf, A., & Al-Akiti, A. (2022). Where the two oceans meet: The theology of Islam and the philosophy of psychiatric medicine in exploring the human self. In *Islam and Biomedicine* (pp. 135–182). Cham: Springer International Publishing.

Zhong, W., Schröder, T., & Bekkering, J. (2022). Biophilic design in architecture and its contributions to health, well-being, and sustainability: A critical review. *Frontiers of Architectural Research*, *11*(1), 114–141. https://doi.org/10.1016/j.foar.2021.07.006

7 Conclusion

Merve Nursoy-Demir and Rania Awaad

Concluding Remarks on the Maristān Model of Holistic Care

Maristāns were mediaeval Islāmic institutions that were systematic, empirically driven, long-lasting, and self-sustaining healthcare facilities. They were also amongst the first hospitals, if not the first, in human history to medicinise mental health treatment and use a holistic model to treat psychiatric patients. In this book, our mission is to unearth the historical contributions of maristāns centuries after they were forgotten. We suggest that modern-day Islāmic Psychology (IP) clinical settings adopt the maristān model of holistic care based on the efficacy and ingenuity of this incredible model of holistic healing centres that became a flagship institution of the Islamic Civilisation. In this closing chapter, we provide an overview of historical maristāns and of the maristān model of holistic care. We can summarise the important lessons gained from this in-depth analysis of maristāns in the following points:

Intention, Motivation, and Foundation

1 The Islāmic inspiration and motivation that inspired the creation of these holistic healing centres make maristāns particularly relevant to modern IP clinical practice. Islāmic teachings about health and healing, knowledge seeking and scientific inquiry, charity and legacy, to name a few, were the driving forces behind every maristān we studied, irrespective of the time or location of their construction. The impact of these Islāmic teachings spans from the waqfīyyah documents that guaranteed ongoing charitable care (Chapter 1) to the meticulous attention to detail and spiritual symbolism in the carvings adorning even the doorways of these buildings (Chapter 5).
2 Across the vast geography of the Muslim world, from Spain to South Asia, and lasting over 1,000 years from the 8th century to the 19th century (Chapter 2), the founders of these maristāns had the explicit motivation of gaining the riḍah (i.e., contentment, approval, and satisfaction) of Allāh (ﷻ) by establishing institutions that embodied the Islāmic

DOI: 10.4324/9781003329589-7

principle of ongoing charity (ṣadaqah jāriyah). Even when political or personal motivations came into the picture, the primary aim remained the acceptance of God (Chapter 1). We argue that the output of such strong motivation, rooted in Islam, was a significant factor in the success of the maristāns' centuries-long service of excellence.

3 Sharing common fundamental characteristics despite being in diverse Muslim lands and under numerous rulers, maristāns were based on a model of intentional medical infrastructure. They were all established through the waqf system of finance (Chapter 3), had similar patronages with similar intentions, operated with medical knowledge (i.e., using scientific and empirical methods, yet not neglecting spiritual and rational methods of inquiry), and, most importantly, offered medicalised psychiatric treatment for the mentally ill. Hence, maristāns were pioneers in psychiatric care and can be understood as a premodern system of mental healthcare.

Financial and Administrative Management

4 Based on the Islāmically inspired waqf-based financial system, maristāns were able to remain well-funded and self-sustaining medical institutions for centuries. Philanthropic donors sponsored endowments comprised of sustainable resources that then generated income that was carefully managed, allowing maristāns to provide holistic healthcare free of charge, usually targeting the portion of society that were most in need (Chapter 3).

5 Surviving *waqfīyyah* documents reveal thoroughly outlined roles, income sources, and expenditures, resulting in centuries of preserved quality and careful supervision in maristāns. The administrations that governed these *awqāf* were comprised of diverse representatives, creating a system of checks and balances. The combination of founders, trustees, auditors, legal and medical authorities, and state agencies contributed to the success of a well-functioning maristān system (Chapter 3).

Attitude Towards Mental Health

6 The Islāmic tradition inspired and incentivised the inclusion, care, and treatment of the mentally ill. Socially, people with psychiatric illnesses were visible in everyday life in Islāmic societies, cared for and accepted as part of the community (Dols, 1992; Tunaboylu-İkiz, 1999). Legally, the voice of those with mental illness was heard in courts; they were given the right to defend themselves and remain under the family's custody/care without being forced into institutionalised care unless they were dangerous to the community (Sarı, 2016). Medically, mental illnesses were usually defined as part of the brain and head diseases and were described empirically rather than morally or religiously (Sarı, 2020).

Treatment Team

7 Treatment in mediaeval maristāns was delivered by a multidisciplinary team led by physicians and included medical students, pharmacists, nurses, dieticians, *murāfiqīn* (companions), spiritual advisors (akin to chaplains today), entertainers and healers, and individuals who helped manage the needs of patients both inside and outside of the hospital—similar to hospital social workers today—(Awaad et al., 2019). Collectively, this diverse team addressed the mind, body, and spirit-based needs of the patients and was pivotal in providing holistic patient care and hospital management. *Waqfīyyah* documents outlined stringent standards for maristān physicians, emphasising their management skills, compassion, and ability to design comprehensive treatment plans. These physicians were often polymaths, addressing various illnesses, including mental health, and possessed competency in psychological matters in order to deliver adequate care (Chapter 4).

8 Maristāns had diverse and specialised staff beyond medical providers, with some hospitals employing musicians for therapeutic purposes, for example. Ancillary staff such as security guards, clerks, cooks, and sanitation workers were recruited according to patient requirements. The kitchen staff, including pantrymen and cooks, played a crucial role in customising meals according to patients' medical conditions and aligning the food service with patients' prescriptions, emphasising quality and variety. Imams, muezzins, and Qur'ān reciters were also brought in for spiritual support, offering patients the freedom to engage in religious practices (Chapter 4).

Therapeutic Interventions

9 Psychiatric conditions were treated in maristāns using a holistic treatment plan that was informed by a multiplex understanding of human ontology through which health and illness were defined as a combination of biological, psychological, social, and spiritual factors. Accordingly, the personal characteristics interacted with horizontal (intrapersonal, interpersonal, familial, communal, and environmental) and vertical (metaphysical and divine) relationships to constitute holistic well-being or disturbance (Chapter 6).

10 In alignment with this multidimensional human ontology model, the treatment modalities used in maristāns were quite diverse and ranged from therapeutic diets, music therapy, and behavioural and talk therapies to medications and cauterisation. Physicians exercised caution to avoid harming patients, following the Islāmic medical principle of mimicking the body's natural response and restoring homeostasis. Gradual and careful transitions in treatment, starting with non-invasive interventions, were preferred, emphasising the restoration of a healthy diet and circadian rhythm as initial steps to recovery (Chapter 4).

Architecture and Design

11. The physical built environment of the maristāns—which were often located in city centres as part of larger kulliyah complexes alongside mosques, *madāris*, *ḥammāmāt*, soup kitchens, and bazaars—was an active agent in a patient's holistic healing process. The architectural design of maristāns also played an important role through their balanced and curative features of orientation, connection, scale, and symbolism. The incorporation of natural elements and symbolic design in maristāns, which aligns perfectly with the modern concept of biophilic design, contributed to their therapeutic healing properties (Chapter 5).
12. The very structure of the maristān contributed to the well-being of patients by targeting their souls through symbolism that indicated the *Tawhîd* (oneness of Allāh [ﷻ]). Specifically aimed to restore patients to their innate state of balance (*fiṭrah*), the symbolism found in maristāns' architectural designs was rooted in principles of Divine Architecture found in nature. Traditional Muslim architects considered nature both an artistic muse and a healing source guided by philosophical reasoning. At the same time, Qur'ānic teachings highlighted the interconnected primordial states of humans and nature, suggesting that encounters with nature could restore balance.

Concluding Remarks on Maristāns as a Clinical Model for Holistic Care

In this book, we propose a blueprint of the maristān model for holistic care that aims to provide a set of practical guidelines for the modern-day IP field that is based on the extraordinary features of historical maristāns (Chapter 6). Accordingly, the maristān model:

1. Emphasises the Islāmic concept of intentionality, suggesting that the clinician's *niyyah* (intention) functions as a seed that influences the clinical outcome. Along with empirical and rational sources of knowledge, there is a deep regard in IP practice for the unseen intentions behind one's actions and clinical interventions. By aligning with the Islāmic principles of intentionality and *iḥsān*, it is expected that the efficacy of the clinician's efforts in the present and the hereafter will be enhanced.
2. Suggests a community-centred approach inspired by the historical maristāns, such as utilising Islāmically inspired funding mechanisms that incorporate the use of *awqāf* and zakat funds to address modern mental healthcare gaps. This includes advocating for tax-deductible, non-profit mental healthcare clinics that are accessible to and centred within Muslim communities. Taking inspiration from the *kulliyyah* complex system, building modern maristāns in collaboration with and adjacent to other

Islāmic institutions, such as mosques and *madāris*, makes the maristān more accessible and trusted by Muslim communities. The maristān model underscores the need to redirect zakat and charity funds to the building of holistic mental healthcare centres in order to address an unmet issue in modern-day Muslim communities and, in doing so, dismantle cultural stigmas that have become barriers to accessing much-needed mental healthcare.

3 Addresses self-sustainability by suggesting that endowed properties, such as stocks or lands, are needed as a steady source of income for modern mental healthcare institutions. The maristān model is up against the complexity of current financing structures that must be studied and negotiated vis a vis traditional Islāmic funding structures. We believe integrating both financial structures is possible (as exemplified by the Maristān Clinic in California, USA) and advocate for creating more community-driven institutions.
4 Suggests giving patients self-agency, reflecting historical practices that prioritised informed consent and patient self-determination—including mentally ill patients.
5 Adopts a comprehensive clinical approach, addressing the interconnected physiological, psychological, cognitive, social, and spiritual dimensions of an individual's well-being. Accordingly, the maristān model is multiplex in its theoretical framework, acknowledging the intertwined external and internal factors influencing psychological problems, such as geography, temperament, daily routines, and social influences, while incorporating aspects of an individual's body, mind, heart, and soul into the diagnostic and treatment processes. Hence, in current IP practice, clinicians are urged to incorporate this multidimensional understanding, moving beyond primarily individualistic conventional psychotherapeutic frameworks in order to address patients holistically.
6 Emphasises the need for a multidisciplinary treatment team, including clinicians, physicians, pharmacists, therapists, nurses, dieticians, chaplains, students, and social workers, all collaborating to intervene and address various dimensions of health and well-being.
7 Advocates for the incorporation of overlooked clinical tools and alternative healing methods in order to achieve genuinely holistic care. Examples include incorporating temperament theories, self-help tools, indigenous Islāmic spiritual practices such as various forms of *ḏhikr*, *tafakkur* (contemplative meditation), and Qur'ānic recitation, as well as therapies that heal each of the five senses such as integrating aroma, somatic/body-based, sound/music, art/colour, and talk therapies into contemporary clinical practice.
8 Emphasises the importance of indirect elements (physical setting, administrative structure, cleanliness, attitudes of the staff, quality of the food served, etc.) in addition to the direct agents (medical care team,

medications, and treatments) in contributing to the healing process. The maristān model pays close attention to the effect of tactile experiences, as well as visual, auditory and olfactory stimuli, on holistic well-being.

9 Offers an architecturally aesthetic and moderately sized building that eschews the overwhelming scale of modern hospitals. The design of maristān-inspired clinics balances accessibility and privacy while emphasising simplicity, ease of navigation, familiarity, and security. The biophilic approach incorporates natural elements such as greenery, water fountains, and natural scents and is built using sustainable materials. The maristān model suggests that design elements such as curvilinearity, greenery, atriums, and a centralised courtyard can support a holistic healing experience in modern clinical settings.
10 Emphasises psychoeducation as part of the healing process by educating clinicians in training, patients seeking care within the maristan, but also the general community about mental well-being. This commitment is in line with the Islamic mandate to learn, seek knowledge and educate others. Reviving the historical kulliyyah model of maristans that once housed on-site medical schools, clinical apprenticeships, and teaching programmes that were open to the general community will greatly benefit those seeking healing within as well as beyond the walls of the maristan.
11 Targets spiritual growth for both the clinician and the patient by fostering a connection with the divine through the symbolism found in the maristān's art and architecture. The maristān's very architectural design invites individuals to reflect upon a more profound, metaphysical understanding of their existence.
12 Is fundamentally God-centred such that the relationship of an individual with their Creator is defined as the core of holistic well-being. This perspective carries the psychotherapeutic relationship and its subjects (the clinician and the patient) into the metaphysical realm, expanding the interventions' healing potential.
13 Underscores the importance of personal and professional *akhlāq* (ethics) among clinical specialists. This encourages contemporary IP clinicians to prioritise both professional development and personal growth, considering moral maturity as integral to clinical competence. This approach suggests that integrating Islāmic practices and healing methods into the therapeutic space requires an IP clinician to consider the impact of their inner state, morality, and spirituality on the psychotherapeutic process. We cannot emphasise enough the dangers of clinicians offering clinical care without simultaneously working on enhancing their own holistic well-being.

Limitations

There are several potential limitations in our research. Mainly, as a result of relying heavily on historical sources, our work may be subject to biases, inaccuracies, or limitations given the incomplete nature of historical accounts and records. We tried to neutralise these biases or inaccuracies by extrapolating information from multiple, diverse sources in various languages. Nevertheless, caution is advised as for any volume handling historical depictions.

Another limitation of our work is the lack of primary sources that directly describe treatments used to treat mental illnesses in the maristāns. Due to the historical nature of these maristāns, detailed treatment modalities or patient records produced directly by physicians were challenging to locate. Eyewitness accounts and historical texts on theoretical medicine provided plausible hints about the actual treatments, we rarely located hospital records or physician medical notes that outlined exact clinical interventions. Even though historical accounts describe how physicians regularly logged patient records, the manuscripts that directly reported the outcomes of treatments and interventions used were scarce. One of the main reasons for the scarcity of primary sources is the significant destruction of Islāmicate archives due to recurring episodes of wars and invasions—both recent and ancient—in the Near and Middle East regions (Paul, 2018; Qureshi, 2009). For instance, the world-famous libraries of the Islamic heritage and knowledge centres in Baghdad, such as Bayt al-Hikmah, were destroyed during the Mongol invasions in the 13th century (Iqbal, 2021).

Another potential limitation is the over-generalisation of historical information. Due to the broad geographical and temporal expanse during which maristāns flourished, our sources spread across diverse geographical regions, languages and time periods. This brings inevitable variance to some extent based on local cultures, conditions, and temporal differences. It is crucial to keep in mind that the resources available, services provided, or maristāns mentioned have changed over time. While many patterns seemed consistent across all surveyed sources, further research is required to specify differentiating characteristics between maristāns or trends of changes in a given location. Thus, the reader should responsibly consume the intellectual material provided here by treating it as one interpretation and an attempt to consolidate extensive information.

One remaining puzzle piece that needs to be addressed is the downfall of the maristān system. Because of the limitation of space and the need to utilise historical information at hand to create a working clinical model for today, the focus remains on the active and functional periods and aspects of maristāns. As such, the history of the maristāns' demolishment and the reasons for this system's decline are omitted in the current volume. However, it is critical to understand the dysfunction of a system as much as its successes before utilising it as a model for future clinical practice. Key aspects such as colonisation, mismanagement of endowment funds, the advent of technology, in addition to other pertinent contributing factors should be further examined in future analyses.

Future Studies

In addition to the aforementioned gaps in the existing literature, more interdisciplinary studies are needed to further unearth archival sources and translate them for the benefit of the current IP field. There is more to discover in the long-forgotten archives of Islāmic history; however, this task is beyond the capacity of one lab or a small group of specialists. Well-funded, extensive multidisciplinary research is required to dig deep enough in order to provide a more complete picture. This requires the collective work of a strong team of psychologists, psychiatrists, social scientists (e.g., historians, sociologists, anthropologists), and Islāmic scholars. We highlight the importance of interdisciplinary research given that IP as a field is built upon a multiplex understanding of the human psyche.

In addition to interdisciplinary attempts at uncovering historical material, one crucial direction for future studies is testing historical treatment methods and diagnostic frameworks that were used in the maristāns. The aim is not to romanticise but rather to examine the utility of these holistic healing methods that were used for centuries to treat psychiatric patients and were remarkably ahead of their time. As such, assessing traditional mental health interventions that were once used in maristāns, such as *maqam* therapy, herbal medications, specialised diets, and temperament analysis, as just a few examples of the many diverse healing methods used in historical maristans, may prove to be beneficial and enriching tools for holistic healing in modern IP clinical practice.

Conclusion

There is an awakening taking place in the mental health field today, an acknowledgement that modern clinical interventions are only partially treating our mental health. Often limited to cognitive or behavioural aspects of well-being, these treatments fall short of appreciating the complex and multiplex nature of the human psyche. This is often troubling to Muslims, as we believe that the human being is created with a multidimensional existence and, thus, each of those dimensions must be treated collectively and holistically. Psychotherapy and psychopharmacology are valuable methods, yet they remain unidimensional attempts at addressing well-being (Awaad, 2022). Since the understanding of the multiplex nature of human potential remains limited with modern-day frameworks and tools at hand, we need alternative models of holistic healing that will provide a broader wellness experience to those experiencing mental health challenges. In the post-pandemic era, the need for nuanced, sophisticated, and multidimensional healing models is more urgent than ever before. Hence, it is imperative that mental health professionals expand their conceptualisation of health and illness, and the maristān model of mental healthcare can provide excellent inspiration.

Islāmic teachings were the primary source of inspiration, the impetus for creating a model that historically led to holistic healing in maristāns. The false dichotomy of separating religious and 'secular' sciences that is a commonplace belief held by clinicians today did not exist in the era of the maristāns. The Islāmic tradition did not stifle intellectual or technological progress but rather sponsored and encouraged the spread of knowledge. We argue that the field of human psychology will only be complete enough to provide in-depth healing not only to Muslims, but to all people in general, when the Islāmic conceptualisations of human ontology, health, and illness are bridged to modern clinical practice. Knowing that such comprehensive and holistic mental healthcare was a reality in the not-so-distant past must inspire IP professionals to continue working for the rooted revival of the maristān model.

Today, the field of IP stands at a crossroads: how much of the Islāmic heritage are modern practitioners ready to incorporate confidently into their current clinical practice? Or should we wait for another half-century to see if the mainstream mental health field continues its slow but inevitable progress towards a more holistic approach that incorporates the spiritual and metaphysical aspects of care, and only then do we, as IP practitioners, follow in its footsteps? The latter would certainly be ironic given that Muslims have been the forerunners of the holistic maristān model for centuries. IP practitioners should feel empowered to take the next steps as rightful inheritors of a heritage that has already proven itself capable of addressing mental health concerns using an interdisciplinary and multifaceted approach.

At the time of writing this book's first edition, efforts are already underway to revive the maristān model, and, of course, the namesake for this effort is none other than Maristān—a holistic mental health not-for-profit organisation located in California. Maristān aims to provide spiritually and religiously congruent psychotherapeutic services that bridge cutting-edge psychological knowledge with holistic healing methods inherited from its namesake. Its first healing centre is attached to one of the largest mosques in the San Francisco Bay Area where it is located, similar to the *kulliyyah* model of historical maristāns. Moreover, Maristān works hand in hand with the Muslim Mental Health and Islāmic Psychology Lab at Stanford University School of Medicine to produce evidence-based research that informs its clinical work and community-based psychoeducational programmes. This collaboration increases the capacity of Maristān as a holistic healing centre to serve local, national, and global Muslim communities, similar to how the historical medical *madāris* used to operate in collaboration with the maristāns.

Reclaiming a legacy is never easy, nor has our attempt at rewriting the narrative of an otherwise Eurocentric history of psychology been either. We pray that the ultimate aim of this book has been met: to provide a blueprint for the first and most comprehensive model for mental healthcare known in human history and begin to bridge this model to modern clinical practice. In so doing, we pray that it serves as an inspiration to the modern-day IP practitioner as well as the general field of psychology, as there is no better way to heal our individual and collective mental well-being than to do so holistically.

References

Awaad, R., Mohammad, A., Elzamzamy, K., Fereydooni, S., & Gamar, M. (2019). Mental health in the Islāmic golden era: The historical roots of modern psychiatry. *Islamophobia and Psychiatry: Recognition, Prevention, and Treatment*, 3–17. https://doi.org/10.1007/978-3-030-00512-2_1

Awaad, R. (July 31, 2022). Maristans and multiplexity: Islāmic psychology in practice. In: *Conference Presentation Towards a Multiplex Relational Theory of Action: Why Do People Do What They Do?* Istanbul, Turkiye. https://fs.ihu.edu.tr/siteler/ihu.edu.tr/6298af6b4cb03/files/conference-program-pdf.pdf

Dols, M. W. (1992). *Majnūn: The Madman in Medieval Islāmic society*. Clarendon Press.

Iqbal, M. (2021). The impact of mongol invasion on the Muslim world and the political, economic and social ramifications. *Economic and Social Ramifications*. https://dx-doi-org.stanford.idm.oclc.org/10.2139/ssrn.3899594

Qureshi, F. (2009). An assessment of the destruction and rehabilitation of libraries during a period of armed conflict: A case study of iraq's libraries. 2003 Doctoral dissertation, University of Wales. https://eprints.soas.ac.uk/id/eprint/7245

Paul, J. (2018). Archival practices in the Muslim world prior to 1500. *Manuscripts and Archives: Comparative Views on Record-Keeping*, *11*, 339. https://library.oapen.org/bitstream/handle/20.500.12657/27417/9783110541397.pdf?sequence=1#page=353

Sarı, N. (2016). *A Review of Ottoman Court Records on Mental Diseases*. https://www.academia.edu/45426699/A_Review_of_Ottoman_Court_Records_on_Mental_Diseases

Sarı, N. (2020, January 1). Osmanlı Darüşşifasında Tedavi. In *Afyon and Istanbul International Turkish-Islamic Medical History and Ethics Congresses (2018–2019) Proceedings Book, Konya*. https://www.academia.edu/46571791/Osmanl%C4%B1_Dar%C3%BC%C5%9F%C5%9Fifas%C4%B1nda_Tedavi

Tunaboylu-İkiz, T. (1999). Türk psikiyatri tarihi ve psikanalizin yeri. *Psikoloji Çalışmaları*, 21, 159–168.

Index

Note: **Bold** page numbers refer to tables; *italic* page numbers refer to figures and page numbers followed by "n" denote endnotes.

FSC
www.fsc.org
MIX
Papier | Fördert
gute Waldnutzung
FSC® C083411

Kolibri 360 GmbH
Ferdinand-Jühlke-Straße 7
99095 Erfurt, Deutschland
produktsicherheit@kolibri360.de